FTCE Exceptional Student Education K-12 Practice Test Kit

By: Sharon Wynne, M.S.

XAMonline, Inc.
Boston

Copyright © 2014 XAMonline, Inc.
All rights reserved. No part of the material protected by this copyright notice may be reproduced or utilized in any form or by any means, electronic or mechanical, including photocopying, recording or by any information storage and retrievable system, without written permission from the copyright holder.

To obtain permission(s) to use the material from this work for any purpose including workshops or seminars, please submit a written request to:

XAMonline, Inc.
21 Orient Avenue
Melrose, MA 02176
Email: info@xamonline.com
Web: www.xamonline.com
Phone:1-800-301-4647
Fax: 617-583-5552

Library of Congress Cataloging-in-Publication Data

Wynne, Sharon A.
FTCE Exceptional Student Education K-12 Practice Test Kit: Teacher Certification / Sharon A. Wynne 1st edition   ISBN: 978-1-60787-400-3
1. FTCE Exceptional Student Education   2. Study Guides.   3. FTCE
4. Teachers' Certification & Licensure   5. Careers

Disclaimer:
The opinions expressed in this publication are the sole works of XAMonline and were created independently from the State Department of Education or other testing affiliates.

Sample test questions are developed by XAMonline and are not former tests.
XAMonline makes no claims nor guarantees teacher candidates a passing score.

Printed in the United States of America
FTCE Exceptional Student Education K-12 Practice Test Kit
ISBN: 978-1-60787-400-3

FTCE Exceptional Student Education K-12 Practice Test Kit
Table of Contents

Pre-Test 4

Answer Key 35

Rigor Table 36

Rationales 37

Post-Test 98

Answer Key 129

Rigor Table 130

Rationales 131

Pre-test

1. A ruling pertaining to the use of evaluation procedures later consolidated in Public Law 94 – 142 resulted from which court case listed?
   (Average Rigor) (Skill 1.1)

   A. Diana v. the State Board of Education (1970)
   B. Wyatt v. Stickney
   C. Larry P. v. Riles
   D. PASE v. Hannon

2. Included in data brought to the attention of Congress regarding the evaluation procedures for education of students with disabilities was the fact that:
   (Easy) (Skill 1.1)

   A. There were a large number of children and youths with disabilities in the United States.
   B. Many children with disabilities were not receiving an appropriate education.
   C. Many parents of children with disabilities were forced to seek services outside of the public realm.
   D. All of the above

3. The Individuals with Disabilities Education Act (IDEA) was signed into law in and later reauthorized through a second revision in what years?
   (Rigorous) (Skill 1.1)

   A. 1975 and 2004
   B. 1980 and 1990
   C. 1990 and 2004
   D. 1995 and 2001

4. How was the training of special education teachers changed by the No Child Left Behind Act of 2002?
   (Rigorous) (Skill 1.1)

   A. It required all special education teachers to be certified in reading and math.
   B. It required all special education teachers to take the same coursework as general education teachers.
   C. If a special education teacher is teaching a core subject, he or she must meet the standard of a highly-qualified teacher in that subject.
   D. All of the above

5. **The No Child Left Behind Act (NCLB) affected students with Limited English Proficiency (LEP) by:**
(Rigorous) (Skill 1.1)

   A. Requiring these students to demonstrate English Language Proficiency before a High School Diploma is granted.
   B. Providing allowances for schools not to require them to take and pass state Reading Exams (RCTs) if the students were enrolled in U.S. schools for less than a year.
   C. Providing allowances for these students to opt out of state math tests if the students were enrolled in a U.S. school for less than one year.
   D. Both B and C

6. **Which of the following is a specific change of language in the IDEA?**
(Rigorous) (Skill 1.1)

   A. The term "Disorder" changed to "Disability."
   B. The term "Children" changed to "Children and Youth."
   C. The term "Handicapped" changed to "Impairments."
   D. The term "Handicapped" changed to "With Disabilities."

7. **Which component changed with the reauthorization of the Education for all Handicapped Children Act of 1975 (EHA) 1990 EHA Amendment?**
(Rigorous) (Skill 1.1)

   A. Specific terminology
   B. Due process protections
   C. Non-discriminatory reevaluation procedures
   D. Individual education plans

8. **The definition of assistive technology devices was amended in the IDEA reauthorization of 2004 to exclude what?**
(Average Rigor) (Skill 1.1)

   A. iPods and other hand-held devices
   B. Computer enhanced technology
   C. Surgically implanted devices
   D. Braille and/or special learning aids

9. **Which is untrue about the Americans with disabilities Act (ADA)?**
(Rigorous) (Skill 1.1)

   A. It was signed into law by President Bush the same year as IDEA.
   B. It reauthorized the discretionary programs of EHA.
   C. It gives protection to all people on the basis of race, sex, national origin, and religion.
   D. It guarantees equal opportunities to persons with disabilities in employment, public accommodations, transportation, government services, and telecommunications.

10. **The opportunity for persons with disabilities to live as close to the normal as possible describes:**
(Average Rigor) (Skill 1.1)

   A. Least restrictive environment
   B. Normalization
   C. Mainstreaming
   D. Deinstitutionalization

11. **Requirements for evaluations were changed in IDEA 2004 to reflect that no 'single' assessment or measurement tool can be used to determine special education qualification, furthering that there was a disproportionate representation of what types of students?**
(Average Rigor) (Skill 1.1)

   A. Disabled
   B. Foreign
   C. Gifted
   D. Minority and bilingual

12. **What determines whether a person is entitled to protection under Section 504?**
(Average Rigor) (Skill 1.1)

   A. The individual must meet the definition of a person with a disability.
   B. The person must be able to meet the requirements of a particular program in spite of his or her disability.
   C. The school, business, or other facility must be the recipient of federal funding assistance.
   D. All of the above

13. **Legislation in Public Law 94 – 142 attempts to:**
    (Rigorous) (Skill 1.1)

    A. Match the child's educational needs with appropriate educational services.
    B. Include parents in the decisions made about their child's education.
    C. Establish a means by which parents can provide input.
    D. All of the above

14. **Effective transition was included in:**
    (Rigorous) (Skill 1.1)

    A. President Bush's 1990 State of the Union Message
    B. Public Law 101-476
    C. Public Law 95-207
    D. Both A and B

15. **The Free Appropriate Public Education (FAPE) describes Special Education and related services as?**
    (Easy) (Skill 1.2)

    A. Public expenditure and standard to the state educational agency.
    B. Provided in conformity with each student's individualized education program, if the program is developed to meet requirements of the law.
    C. Including preschool, elementary, and/or secondary education in the state involved.
    D. All of the above

16. Jane is a third grader. Mrs. Smith, her teacher, noted that Jane was having difficulty with math and reading assignments. The results from recent diagnostic tests showed a strong sight vocabulary and strength in computational skills, but a weakness in comprehending what she read. This weakness was apparent in mathematical word problems as well. The multi-disciplinary team recommended placement in a special education resource room for learning disabilities two periods each school day. For the remainder of the school day, her placement will be: *(Easy) (Skill 1.2)*

    A. In the regular classroom
    B. At a special school
    C. In a self-contained classroom
    D. In a resource room for mental retardation

17. Which of the following must be provided in a written notice to parents when proposing a child's educational placement? *(Average Rigor) (Skill 1.2)*

    A. A list of parental due process safeguards
    B. A list of current test scores
    C. A list of persons responsible for the child's education
    D. A list of academic subjects the child has passed

18. Zero Reject requires all children with disabilities be provided with what? *(Average Rigor) (Skill 1.2)*

    A. Total exclusion of functional exclusion
    B. Adherence to the annual local education agency (LEA) reporting
    C. Free, appropriate public education
    D. Both B and C

19. Students who receive special services in a regular classroom with consultation generally have academic and/or social-interpersonal performance deficits at which level of severity?
 (Easy) (Skill 1.2)

   A. Mild
   B. Moderate
   C. Severe
   D. Profound

20. The greatest number of students receiving special services is enrolled primarily in:
 (Average Rigor) (Skill 1.2)

   A. The regular classroom
   B. The resource room
   C. Self-contained classrooms
   D. Special schools

21. The most restrictive environment in which an individual might be placed and receive instruction is that of:
 (Easy) (Skill 1.2)

   A. Institutional setting
   B. Homebound instruction
   C. Special schools
   D. Self-contained special classes

22. The law affects required components of the IEP; elements required by the IEP and the law are:
 (Rigorous) (Skill 1.3)

   A. Present level of academic and functional performance; statement of how the disability affects the student's involvement and progress ;evaluation criteria and timeliness for instructional objective achievement; modifications of accommodations
   B. Projected dates for services initiation with anticipated frequency, location and duration; statement of when parent will be notified; statement of annual goals
   C. Extent to which child will not participate in regular education program; transitional needs for students age 14.
   D. All of the above.

23. **IEPs continue to have multiple sections; one section, present levels, now addresses what?**
(Average Rigor) (Skill 1.3)

   A. Academic achievement and functional performance
   B. English as a second language
   C. Functional performance
   D. Academic achievement

24. **What is true about IDEA? In order to be eligible, a student must:**
(Easy) (Skill 1.4)

   A. Have a medical disability
   B. Have a disability that fits into one of the categories listed in the law
   C. Attend a private school
   D. Be a slow learner

25. **Changes in requirements for Current Levels of performance require:?**
(Average Rigor) (Skill 1.4)

   A. student voice in each Present Level of Performance.
   B. CSE chair must tell parents when child has unrealistic goals.
   C. Parent/Guardian must attend either by phone conference or in person.
   D. Teachers must write post adult outcomes assigning a student to a specific field.

26. **Developmental Disabilities:**
(Rigorous) (Skill 1.4)

   A. Is the categorical name for mental retardation in IDEA
   B. Includes congenital conditions, such as severe Spina Bifida, deafness, blindness, or profound mental retardation
   C. Includes children who contract diseases, such as polio or meningitis, and who are left in an incapacitated functional state
   D. Both B and C

27. **Which of the following goals reflects new IDEA requirements?**
(Rigorous) (Skill 1.3)

   A. Janet wants to be a doctor.
   B. Frank plans to attend the Culinary Institute.
   C. Janet will go to college.
   D. Carmel currently lives independently on her own.

28. **The definition for "Other Health Impaired (OHI)" in IDEA:**
(Rigorous) (Skill 1.4)

   A. Is the definition that accepts heart conditions
   B. Includes deafness, blindness, or profound mental retardation
   C. Includes Autism and PDD
   D. Includes cochlear implants.

29. **Which is an educational characteristic common to students with mild intellectual learning and behavioral disabilities?**
(Easy) (Skill 1.5)

   A. Show interest in schoolwork
   B. Have intact listening skills
   C. Require modification in classroom instruction
   D. Respond better to passive than to active learning tasks

30. **In general, characteristics of students with learning disabilities include:**
(Average Rigor) (Skill 1.5)

   A. A low level of performance in a majority of academic skill areas
   B. Limited cognitive ability
   C. A discrepancy between achievement and potential
   D. A uniform pattern of academic development

31. **Michael's teacher complains that he is constantly out of his seat. She also reports that he has trouble paying attention to what is going on in class for more than a couple of minutes at a time. He appears to be trying, but his writing is often illegible, containing many reversals. Although he seems to want to please, he is very impulsive and stays in trouble with his teacher. He is failing reading, and his math grades, though somewhat better, are still below average. Michael's psychometric evaluation should include assessment for:**
(Average Rigor)(Skill 1.5)

   A. Mild mental retardation
   B. Specific learning disabilities
   C. Mild behavior disorders
   D. Hearing impairment

32. Joey is in a mainstreamed preschool program. One of the means his teacher uses in determining growth in adaptive skills is that of observation. Some questions about Joey's behavior that she might ask include:
(Average Rigor) (Skill 1.5)

   A. Is he able to hold a cup?
   B. Can he call the name of any of his toys?
   C. Can he reach for an object and grasp it?
   D. All of the above

33. Individuals with mental retardation can be characterized as:
(Rigorous) (Skill 1.5)

   A. Often indistinguishable from normal developing children at an early age
   B. Having a higher than normal rate of motor activity
   C. Displaying significant discrepancies in ability levels
   D. Uneducable in academic skills

34. Which of the following statements about children with an emotional/behavioral disorder is true?
(Average Rigor) (Skill 1.5)

   A. They have very high IQs.
   B. They display poor social skills.
   C. They are poor academic achievers.
   D. Both B and C

35. Which behavior would be expected at the mild level of emotional/behavioral disorders?
(Average Rigor) (Skill 1.5)

   A. Attention seeking
   B. Inappropriate affect
   C. Self-Injurious
   D. Poor sense of identity

36. Which of the following is true about autism?
(Rigorous) (Skill 1.5)

   A. It is caused by having cold, aloof, or hostile parents.
   B. Approximately 4 out of 10 people have autism.
   C. It is a separate exceptionality category in IDEA.
   D. It is a form of mental illness.

37. **Autism is a condition characterized by:**
(Easy) (Skill 1.5)

   A. Distorted relationships with others
   B. Perceptual anomalies
   C. Self-stimulation
   D. All of the above

38. **As a separate exceptionality category in IDEA, autism:**
(Average Rigor) (Skill 1.5)

   A. Includes emotional/behavioral disorders as defined in federal regulations
   B. Adversely affects educational performance
   C. Is thought to be a form of mental illness
   D. Is a developmental disability that affects verbal and non-verbal communication

39. **Normality in child behavior is influenced by society's?**
(Average Rigor) (Skill 1.5)

   A. Attitudes and cultural beliefs
   B. Hereditary factors
   C. Prenatal care
   D. Attitudes and Victorian era motto

40. **The CST coordinates and participates in due diligence through what process?**
(Average Rigor) (Skill 1.6)

   A. Child study team meets for the first time without parents.
   B. Teachers take child learning concerns to the school counselor.
   C. School counselor contacts parents for permission to perform screening assessments.
   D. All of the above

41. **Which of the following examples would be considered of highest priority when determining the need for the delivery of appropriate special education and related services?**
(Rigorous) (Skill 1.6)

A. An eight-year-old boy is repeating first grade for the second time and exhibits problems with toileting, gross motor functions, and remembering number and letter symbols. His regular classroom teacher claims the referral forms are too time-consuming and refuses to complete them. He also refuses to make accommodations because he feels every child should be treated alike.
B. A six-year-old girl who has been diagnosed as autistic is placed in a special education class within the local school. Her mother wants her to attend residential school next year even though the girl is showing progress.
C. A ten-year-old girl with profound mental retardation who is receiving education services in a state institution.
D. A twelve-year-old boy with mild disabilities who was placed in a behavior disorders program but displays obvious perceptual deficits (e.g., reversal of letters and symbols and inability to discriminate sounds). He originally was thought to have a learning disability but did not meet state criteria for this exceptionality category based on results of standard scores. He has always had problems with attending to a task and is now beginning to get into trouble during seatwork time. His teacher feels that he will eventually become a real behavior problem. He receives social skills training in the resource room one period a day.

42. **When a student is identified as being at-risk academically or socially what does Federal law hope for first?**
(Rigorous) (Skill 1.6)

   A. Move the child quickly to assessment.
   B. Place the child in special education as soon as possible.
   C. Observe the child to determine what is wrong.
   D. Perform remedial intervention in the classroom.

43. **What do the 9th and 10th Amendments to the U.S. Constitution state about education?**
(Average Rigor) (Skill 1.8)

   A. That education belongs to the people
   B. That education is an unstated power vested in the states
   C. That elected officials mandate education
   D. That education is free

44. **The IDEA states that child assessment is?**
(Average Rigor) (Skill 2.1)

   A. At intervals with teacher discretion
   B. Continuous on a regular basis
   C. Left to the counselor
   D. Conducted annually

45. **Safeguards against bias and discrimination in the assessment of children include:**
(Average Rigor) (Skill 2.2)

   A. The testing of a child in Standard English
   B. The requirement for the use of one standardized test
   C. The use of evaluative materials in the child's native language or other mode of communication
   D. All testing performed by a certified, licensed psychologist

46. **Which is characteristic of group tests?**
(Average Rigor) (Skill 2.3)

   A. Directions are always read to students.
   B. The examiner monitors several students at the same time.
   C. The teacher is allowed to probe students who almost have the correct answer.
   D. Both quantitative and qualitative information may be gathered.

47. For which of the following uses are standardized individual tests MOST appropriate?
    (Rigorous) (Skill 2.3)

    A. Screening students to determine possible need for special education services
    B. Evaluation of special education curricula
    C. Tracking of gifted students
    D. Evaluation of a student for eligibility and placement, or individualized program planning, in special education

48. Which of the following is an advantage of giving informal individual rather than standardized group tests?
    (Easy) (Skill 2.3)

    A. Questions can be modified to reveal a specific student's strategies or misconceptions.
    B. The test administrator can clarify or rephrase questions.
    C. They can be inserted into the class quickly on an as needed basis.
    D. All of the above

49. Mrs. Stokes has been teaching her third grade students about mammals during a recent science unit. Which of the following would be true of a criterion-referenced test she might administer at the conclusion of the unit?
    (Average Rigor) (Skill 2.3)

    A. It will be based on unit objectives.
    B. Derived scores will be used to rank student achievement.
    C. Standardized scores are effective of national performance samples.
    D. All of the above

50. For which of the following purposes is a norm-referenced test LEAST appropriate?
    (Rigorous) (Skill 2.3)

    A. Screening
    B. Individual program planning
    C. Program evaluation
    D. Making placement decisions

51. **Criterion-referenced tests can provide information about:**
    (Rigorous) (Skill 2.3)

    A. Whether a student has mastered prerequisite skills
    B. Whether a student is ready to proceed to the next level of instruction
    C. Which instructional materials might be helpful in covering program objectives
    D. All of the above

52. **Which of the following purposes of testing calls for an informal test?**
    (Average Rigor) (Skill 2.3)

    A. Screening a group of children to determine their readiness for the first reader
    B. Analyzing the responses of a student with a disability to various presentations of content material to see which strategy works.
    C. Evaluating the effectiveness of a fourth-grade math program at the end of its first year of use in a specific school
    D. Determining the general level of intellectual functioning of a class of fifth graders

53. **Which of the following is not a true statement about informal tests?** *(Average Rigor) (Skill 2.3)*

    A. Informal tests are useful in comparing students to others of their age or grade level.
    B. The correlation between curriculum and test criteria is much higher in informal tests.
    C. Informal tests are useful in evaluating an individual's response to instruction.
    D. Informal tests are used to diagnose a student's particular strengths and weaknesses for purposes of planning individual programs.

54. **For which situation might a teacher be apt to select a formal test?**
    (Rigorous) (Skill 2.3)

    A. A pretest for studying world religions
    B. A weekly spelling test
    C. To compare student progress with that of peers of same age or grade level on a national basis
    D. To determine which content objectives outlined on the student's IEP were mastered

55. The Key Math Diagnostic Arithmetic Test is an individually administered test of math skills. It is comprised of fourteen subtests, which are classified into the major math areas of content, operations, and applications for which subtest scores are reported. The test manual describes the population sample upon which the test was normed and reports data pertaining to reliability and validity. In addition, for each item in the test, a behavioral objective is presented. From the description, it can be determined that this achievement test is:
(Rigorous) (Skill 2.3)

   A. Individually administered
   B. Criterion-referenced
   C. Diagnostic
   D. All of the above

56. The best measures of a student's functional capabilities and entry-level skills are:
(Rigorous) (Skill 2.3)

   A. Norm-referenced tests
   B. Teacher-made post-tests
   C. Standardized IQ tests
   D. Criterion-referenced measures

57. One of your students receives a percentile rank of 45 on a standardized test. This indicates that the student's score:
(Rigorous) (Skill 2.4)

   A. Consisted of 45 correct answers
   B. Was at the point above which 45% of the other scores fell
   C. Was at the point below which 45% of the other scores fell
   D. Was below passing

58. Children who write poorly might be given tests that allow oral responses, unless the purpose for giving the test is to:
(Easy) (Skill 2.5)

   A. Assess handwriting skills
   B. Test for organization of thoughts
   C. Answer questions pertaining to math reasoning
   D. Assess rote memory

59. Alternative assessments include all of the following EXCEPT:
(Average Rigor) (Skill 2.5)

   A. Portfolios
   B. Interviews
   C. Textbook chapter tests
   D. Student choice of assessment format

60. **Which of the following is an example of an alternative assessment?**
    (Rigorous) (Skill 2.5)

    A. Testing skills in a "real world" setting in several settings
    B. Pre-test of student knowledge of fractions before beginning wood shop
    C. Answering an essay question that allows for creative thought
    D. A compilation of a series of tests in a portfolio

61. **Acculturation refers to the individual's:**
    (Rigorous) (Skill 2.6)

    A. Gender
    B. Experiential background
    C. Social class
    D. Ethnic background

62. **To which aspect does fair assessment relate?**
    (Easy) (Skill 2.6)

    A. Representation
    B. Acculturation
    C. Language
    D. All of the above

63. **A test that measures students' skill development in academic content areas is classified as an _____ test.**
    (Average Rigor) (Skill 3.1)

    A. Achievement
    B. Aptitude
    C. Adaptive
    D. Intelligence

64. **Which of the following is an example of tactile perception?**
    (Average Rigor) (Skill 3.2)

    A. Making an angel in the snow with one's body
    B. Running a specified course
    C. Identifying a rough surface with eyes closed
    D. Demonstrating aerobic exercises

65. **Which of the following activities best exemplifies a kinesthetic exercise in developing body awareness?**
    (Rigorous) (Skill 3.2)

    A. Touching materials of different textures
    B. Playing a song/movement game like "Looby Loo"
    C. Identifying geometric shapes being drawn on one's back
    D. Making a shadow-box project

66. Which of the following teaching activities is LEAST likely to enhance observational learning in students with special needs?
    (Easy) (Skill 3.2)

    A. A verbal description of the task to be performed, followed by having the children immediately attempt to perform the instructed behavior
    B. A demonstration of the behavior, followed by an immediate opportunity for the children to imitate the behavior
    C. A simultaneous demonstration and explanation of the behavior, followed by ample opportunity for the children to rehearse the instructed behavior
    D. Physically guiding the children through the behavior to be imitated, while verbally explaining the behavior

67. The _____ modality is most frequently used in the learning process.

    (Average Rigor) (Skill 3.2)

    A. Auditory
    B. Visual
    C. Tactile
    D. All of the Above

68. _____ is a method used to increase student engaged learning time by having students teach other students.
    (Easy) (Skill 3.2)

    A. Collaborative learning
    B. Engaged learning time
    C. Allocated learning time
    D. Teacher consultation

69. Some environmental elements that influence the effectiveness of learning styles include all EXCEPT:
    (Easy) (Skill 3.2)

    A. Light
    B. Temperature
    C. Design
    D. Motivation

70. In order for a student to function independently in the learning environment, which of the following must be true?
    (Average Rigor) (Skill 3.2)

    A. The learner must understand the nature of the content.
    B. The student must be able to do the assigned task.
    C. The teacher must communicate performance criteria to the learner.
    D. All of the above

71. **What can a teacher plan that will allow him/her to avoid adverse situations with students?**
(Rigorous) (Skill 3.2)

    A. Instructional techniques
    B. Instructional materials and formats
    C. Physical setting and the Environment
    D. All of the above

72. **John learns best through the auditory channel, so his teacher wants to reinforce his listening skills. Through which of the following types of equipment would instruction be most effectively presented?**
(Easy) (Skill 3.2)

    A. Overhead projector
    B. Cassette player
    C. Microcomputer
    D. Opaque projector

73. **When teaching a student who is predominantly auditory to read, it is best to:**
(Rigorous) (Skill 3.2)

    A. Stress sight vocabulary
    B. Stress phonetic analysis
    C. Stress the shape and configuration of the word
    D. Stress rapid reading

74. **If a student is predominantly a visual learner, he may learn more effectively by:**
(Easy) (Skill 3.2)

    A. Reading aloud while studying
    B. Listening to a cassette tape
    C. Watching a filmstrip
    D. Using body movement

75. **A prerequisite skill is:**
(Average Rigor) (Skill 3.3)

    A. The lowest order skill in a hierarchy of skills needed to perform a specific task
    B. A skill that must be demonstrated before instruction on a specific task can begin
    C. A tool for accomplishing task analysis
    D. The smallest component of any skill

76. **Presentation of tasks can be altered to match the student's rate of learning by:**
(Rigorous) (Skill 3.3)

    A. Describing how much of a topic is presented in one day and how much practice is assigned according to the student's abilities and learning style
    B. Using task analysis, assign a certain number of skills to be mastered in a specific amount of time
    C. Introducing a new task only when the student has demonstrated mastery of the previous task in the learning hierarchy
    D. Both A and C

77. **All of the following are suggestions for altering the presentation of tasks to match the student's rate of learning EXCEPT:**
(Average Rigor) (Skill 3.3)

    A. Teach in several shorter segments of time rather than a single lengthy session.
    B. Continue to teach a task until the lesson is completed in order to provide more time on task.
    C. Watch for nonverbal cues that indicate students are becoming confused, bored, or restless.
    D. Avoid giving students an inappropriate amount of written work.

78. **Which of the following is a good example of a generalization?**
(Rigorous) (Skill 3.3)

    A. Jim has learned to add and is now ready to subtract.
    B. Sarah adds sets of units to obtain a product.
    C. Bill recognizes a vocabulary word on a billboard when traveling.
    D. Jane can spell the word "net" backwards to get the word "ten."

79. The effective teacher varies her instructional presentations and response requirements depending upon:
(Easy) (Skill 3.3)

   A. Student needs
   B. The task at hand
   C. The learning situation
   D. All of the above

80. For which stage of learning would computer software be utilized that allows for continued drill and practice of a skill to achieve accuracy and speed?
(Average Rigor) (Skill 3.3)

   A. Acquisition
   B. Proficiency
   C. Maintenance
   D. Generalization

81. Alan has failed repeatedly in his academic work. He needs continuous feedback in order to experience small, incremental achievements. What type of instructional material would best meet this need?
(Rigorous) (Skill 3.4)

   A. Programmed materials
   B. Audiotapes
   C. Materials with no writing required
   D. Worksheets

82. After purchasing what seemed to be a very attractive new math kit for use with her SLD (specific learning disabled) students, Ms. Davis discovered her students could not use the kit unless she read the math problems and instructions to them, as the readability level was higher than the majority of the students' functional reading capabilities. Which criterion of the materials selection did Ms. Davis most likely fail to consider when selecting this math kit?
(Average Rigor) (Skill 3.4)

   A. Durability
   B. Relevance
   C. Component parts
   D. Price

83. Which of the following questions most directly evaluates the utility of instructional material?
(Rigorous) (Skill 3.4)

   A. Is the cost within budgetary means?
   B. Can the materials withstand handling by students?
   C. Are the materials organized in a useful manner?
   D. Are the needs of the students met by the use of the materials?

84. A money bingo game was designed by Ms. Johnson for use with her middle grade students. Cards were constructed with different combinations of coins pasted on each of the nine spaces. Ms. Johnson called out various amounts of change (e.g., 30 cents), and students were instructed to cover the coin combinations on their cards, which equaled the amount of change (e.g., two dimes and two nickels, three dimes, and so on). The student who had the first bingo was required to add the coins in each of the spaces covered and tell the amounts before being declared the winner. Five of Ms. Johnson's sixth graders played the game during the ten-minute free activity time following math the first day the game was constructed. Which of the following attributes are present in this game in this situation?*(Average Rigor) (Skill 3.4)*

    A. Accompanied by simple, uncomplicated rules
    B. Of brief duration, permitting replay
    C. Age appropriateness
    D. All of the above

85. According to the three tier RTI model described by the Florida Center for Reading Research's (FCRR), students who need a moderate amount of help in one of the five critical areas of reading instruction in a general education class would receive additional reading instruction through the:
    (Average Rigor) (Skill 5.7)

    A. Core reading program
    B. Intensive Intervention program
    C. Modified Reading program
    D. Supplemental reading program

86. Modifications of course material may take the form of:
    (Average Rigor) (Skill 3.5)

    A. Simplifying texts
    B. Parallel curriculum
    C. Taped textbooks
    D. All of the above

87. At which level of mathematics instruction will a child need to spend the most instructional and exploratory time in order to successfully master objectives?
    (Average Rigor) (Skill 3.11)

    A. Symbolic Level
    B. Concept Level
    C. Mastery Level
    D. Connecting Level

88. **Which is a less than ideal example of collaboration in successful inclusion?**
(Rigorous) (Skill 3.6)

   A. Special education teachers are part of the instructional team in a regular classroom.
   B. Special education teachers assist regular education teachers in the classroom.
   C. Teaming approaches are used for problem solving and program implementation.
   D. Regular teachers, special education teachers, and other specialists or support teachers co-teach.

89. **Janice requires occupational therapy and speech therapy services. She is your student. What must you do to insure her services are met?**
(Rigorous) (Skill 3.6)

   A. Watch the services being rendered.
   B. Schedule collaboratively.
   C. Ask for services to be given in a push-in model.
   D. Ask them to train you to give the service.

90. **What can you do to create a good working environment with a classroom assistant?**
(Rigorous) (Skill 3.6)

   A. Plan lessons with the assistant.
   B. Write a contract that clearly defines his/her responsibilities in the classroom.
   C. Remove previously given responsibilities.
   D. All of the above

91. **A paraprofessional has been assigned to assist you in the classroom. What action on the part of the teacher would lead to a poor working relationship?**
(Average Rigor) (Skill 3.6)

   A. Having the paraprofessional lead a small group
   B. Telling the paraprofessional what you expect him/her to do
   C. Defining classroom behavior management as your responsibility alone
   D. Taking an active role in his/her evaluation

92. **Mrs. Freud is a consultant teacher. She has two students with Mr. Ricardo. Mrs. Freud should:**
(Average Rigor) (Skill 3.6)

    A. Co-teach
    B. Spend two days a week in the classroom helping out.
    C. Discuss lessons with the teacher and suggest modifications before class.
    D. Pull her students out for instructional modifications.

93. **In which way is a computer like an effective teacher?**
(Average Rigor) (Skill 3.7)

    A. Provides immediate feedback
    B. Sets the pace at the rate of the average student
    C. Produces records of errors made only
    D. Programs to skill levels at which students at respective chronological ages should be working

94. **A Behavioral Intervention Plan (BIP):**
(Rigorous) (Skill 4.1)

    A. Should be written by a team.
    B. Should be reviewed annually.
    C. Should be written by the teacher who is primarily responsible for the student.
    D. Should consider placement.

95. **Bill talks out in class an average of 15 times an hour. Other youngsters sometimes talk out, but Bill does so at a higher:**
(Easy) (Skill 4.2)

    A. Rate
    B. Intensity
    C. Volume
    D. Degree

96. **Which category of behaviors would most likely be found on a behavior rating scale?**
(Easy) (Skill 4.3)

    A. Disruptive, acting out
    B. Shy, withdrawn
    C. Aggressive (physical or verbal)
    D. All of the above

97. **In establishing your behavior management plan with the students, it is best to:**
(Average Rigor) (Skill 4.3)

    A. Have rules written and in place on day one.
    B. Hand out a copy of the rules to the students on day one.
    C. Have separate rules for each class on day one.
    D. Have students involved in creating the rules on day one.

98. **Bob shows behavior problems like lack of attention, being out of his seat, and talking out. His teacher has kept data on these behaviors and has found that Bob is showing much better self-control since he has been self-managing himself through a behavior modification program. The most appropriate placement recommendation for Bob at this time is probably:**
(Easy) (Skill 4.4)

    A. Any available part-time special education program
    B. The regular classroom solely
    C. A behavior disorders resource room for one period a day
    D. A specific learning disabilities resource room for one period a day

99. **A Behavior Intervention Plan (BIP) is based on the behaviorist assumption that many problem behaviors are:**
(Average Rigor) (Skill 4.4)

    A. Predictable
    B. Observed
    C. Conditioned
    D. Learned

100. **Procedures employed to decrease targeted behaviors include:**
(Rigorous) (Skill 4.4)

    A. Punishment
    B. Negative reinforcement
    C. Shaping
    D. Both A and B

101. **Target behaviors must be:**
(Easy) (Skill 4.4)

    A. Observable
    B. Measurable
    C. Definable
    D. All of the above

102. **The most important step in writing a Functional Behavioral Assessment (FBA) is:**
(Rigorous) (Skill 4.4)

   A. Establish a replacement behavior.
   B. Establish levels of interventions.
   C. Establish antecedents related or causative to the behavior.
   D. Establish assessment periods of FBA effectiveness.

103. **Which description best characterizes primary reinforcers of an edible nature?**
(Average Rigor) (Skill 4.5)

   A. Natural
   B. Unconditioned
   C. Innately motivating
   D. All of the above

104. **Mrs. Chang is trying to prevent satiation from occurring so that her reinforcers will be effective, as she is using a continuous reinforcement schedule. Which of the following ideas would be LEAST effective in preventing satiation?**
(Rigorous) (Skill 4.5)

   A. Use only one type of edible rather than a variety.
   B. Ask for ten vocabulary words rather than twenty.
   C. Give pieces of cereal, bits of fruit, or M&Ms rather than large portions of edibles.
   D. Administer a peanut then a sip of water.

105. **Which tangible reinforcer would Mr. Whiting find to be MOST effective with teenagers?**
(Easy) (Skill 4.5)

   A. Plastic whistle
   B. Winnie-the-Pooh book
   C. Poster of a current rock star
   D. Toy ring

106. **A positive reinforcer is generally effective if it is desired by the student and is:**
    (Easy) (Skill 4.5)

    A. Worthwhile in size
    B. Given immediately after the desired behavior
    C. Given only upon the occurrence of the target behavior
    D. All of the above

107. **Dispensing school supplies is a component associated with which type of reinforcement system?**
    (Average Rigor) (Skill 4.5)

    A. Activity reinforcement
    B. Tangible reinforcement
    C. Token reinforcement
    D. Both B and C

108. **Which type of reinforcement system is most easily generalized into other settings?**
    (Average Rigor) (Skill 4.5)

    A. Social reinforcement
    B. Activity reinforcement
    C. Tangible reinforcement
    D. Token reinforcement

109. **The Carrow Elicited Language Inventory is a test designed to give the examiner diagnostic information about a child's expressive grammatical competence. Which of the following language components is being assessed?**
    (Rigorous) (Skill 5.1)

    A. Phonology
    B. Morphology
    C. Syntax
    D. Both B and C

110. **In the Grammatic Closure subtest of the Illinois Test of Psycholinguistic Abilities, the child is presented with a picture representing statements such as the following: "Here is one die; here are two ____." This test is essentially a test of:**
    (Rigorous) (Skill 5.1)

    A. Phonology
    B. Syntax
    C. Morphology
    D. Semantics

111. Five-year-old Tom continues to substitute the "w" sound for the "r" sound when pronouncing words; therefore, he often distorts words, e.g., "wabbit" for "rabbit" and "wat" for "rat." His articulation disorder is basically a problem in:
(Average Rigor) (Skill 5.1)

   A. Phonology
   B. Morphology
   C. Syntax
   D. Semantics

112. Which of the following is untrue about the ending "er" ?
(Rigorous) (Skill 5.1)

   A. It is an example of a free morpheme.
   B. It represents one of the smallest units of meaning within a word.
   C. It is called an inflectional ending.
   D. When added to a word, it connotes a comparative status.

113. Which component of language involves language content rather than the form of language?
(Rigorous) (Skill 5.1)

   A. Phonology
   B. Morphology
   C. Semantics
   D. Syntax

114. The social skills of students in mental retardation programs are likely to be appropriate for children of their mental age, rather than chronological age. This means that the teacher will need to do all of the following EXCEPT:
(Easy) (Skill 5.2)

   A. Model desired behavior.
   B. Provide clear instructions.
   C. Expect age-appropriate behaviors.
   D. Adjust the physical environment when necessary.

115. Which of the following is a language disorder?
(Average Rigor) (Skill 5.2)

   A. Articulation problems
   B. Stuttering
   C. Aphasia
   D. Excessive Nasality

116. Which of the following is a speech disorder?
(Average Rigor) (Skill 5.2)

   A. Disfluency
   B. Aphasia
   C. Delayed language
   D. Comprehension difficulties

117. Which of the following is an example of cross-modal perception involving integrating visual stimuli to an auditory verbal process?
    (Rigorous) (Skill 5.3)

    A. Following spoken directions
    B. Describing a picture
    C. Finding certain objects in pictures
    D. Both B and C

118. Matthew's conversational speech is adequate, but when he tries to speak before a group of more than two listeners, his speech becomes mumbling and halting. Which of the following activities would be LEAST helpful in strengthening Matthew's self-expression skills?
    (Rigorous) (Skill 5.3)

    A. Having him participate in show-and-tell time
    B. Asking him comprehension questions about a story that was read to the class
    C. Having him recite a poem in front of the class, with two other children
    D. Asking him to tell a joke to the rest of the class

119. All of the modes listed below are primary categories of Augmentative Alternative Communication EXCEPT:
    (Easy) (Skill 5.4)

    A. Wheelchairs
    B. Graphical communication boards
    C. Eye gaze techniques
    D. Sign language

120. A functional curriculum includes:
    (Average Rigor) (Skill 6.1)

    A. Regents curriculum
    B. Life skills
    C. Remedial academics
    D. Vocational placement

121. Donna has been labeled "learning disabled" since second grade and has developed a fear of not being able to keep up with her peers. She has just entered middle school with a poor self-concept and often acts out to cover up her fear of failure. What is the most appropriate action her teacher can take when Donna exhibits minor inappropriate behavior?
(Rigorous) (Skill 6.1)

   A. Ignore the behavior unless it is too dangerous or distracting.
   B. Praise her for her correct behavior and responses.
   C. Discuss the inappropriate behavior tactfully and in private.
   D. All of the above.

122. Which of the following is the first step you should take to prepare to teach preparation for social situations?
(Average Rigor) (Skill 6.1)

   A. Allow students to plan events.
   B. Lecture.
   C. Anticipate possible problems.
   D. Take your students to the anticipated setting.

123. Children with disabilities are LEAST likely to improve their social-interpersonal skills by:
(Rigorous) (Skill 6.1)

   A. Developing sensitivity to other people
   B. Making behavioral choices in social situations
   C. Developing social maturity
   D. Talking with their sister or brother

124. When you need to evaluate a student's work ethics, you should give what assessment?
(Rigorous) (Skill 6.2)

   A. Naturalistic
   B. Dynamic
   C. Performance-based
   D. Criterion-referenced

125. One of the most important goals of the special education teacher is to foster and create with the student:
(Easy) (Skill 6.3)

   A. Handwriting skills
   B. Self-advocacy
   C. An increased level of reading
   D. Logical reasoning

126. In career education, specific training and preparation required for the world of work occurs during the phase of:
(Average Rigor) (Skill 7.1)

    A. Career awareness
    B. Career exploration
    C. Career preparation
    D. Daily living and personal-social interaction

127. The transition activities that have to be addressed, unless the IEP team finds them uncalled for, are:
(Average Rigor) (Skill 7.2)

    A. Instruction
    B. Community experiences
    C. The development of objectives related to employment and other post-school areas
    D. All of the above

128. The most important member of the transition team is the:
(Easy) (Skill 7.3)

    A. Parent
    B. Student
    C. Secondary personnel
    D. Postsecondary personnel

129. Vocational training programs are based on all of the following ideas EXCEPT:
(Average Rigor) (Skill 7.4)

    A. Students obtain career training from elementary through high school.
    B. Students acquire specific training in job skills prior to exiting school.
    C. Students need specific training and supervision in applying skills learned in school to requirements in job situations.
    D. Students obtain needed instruction and field-based experiences that help them to be able to work in specific occupations.

130. **What is MOST descriptive of vocational training in special education?** *(Easy) (Skill 7.4)*

   A. Trains students in intellectual disabilities solely.
   B. Segregates students with and without disabilities in vocational training programs.
   C. Only includes students capable of moderate supervision.
   D. Instruction focuses upon self-help skills, social-interpersonal skills, motor skills, rudimentary academic skills, simple occupational skills, and lifetime leisure and occupational skills

Answer Key: Pre-test

1.	A	45.	C	89.	B
2.	D	46.	B	90.	A
3.	C	47.	D	91.	C
4.	C	48.	D	92.	C
5.	A	49.	A	93.	A
6.	D	50.	B	94.	A
7.	A	51.	A	95.	A
8.	C	52.	B	96.	D
9.	B	53.	A	97.	D
10.	B	54.	C	98.	B
11.	D	55.	D	99.	D
12.	D	56.	D	100.	A
13.	D	57.	C	101.	D
14.	D	58.	A	102.	C
15.	D	59.	C	103.	D
16.	A	60.	A	104.	A
17.	A	61.	B	105.	C
18.	C	62.	D	106.	D
19.	A	63.	A	107.	A
20.	A	64.	C	108.	A
21.	A	65.	B	109.	C
22.	D	66.	A	110.	C
23.	A	67.	D	111.	A
24.	B	68.	A	112.	A
25.	A	69.	D	113.	C
26.	D	70.	D	114.	C
27.	C	71.	D	115.	C
28.	A	72.	B	116.	A
29.	C	73.	B	117.	B
30.	C	74.	C	118.	B
31.	B	75.	B	119.	A
32.	D	76.	D	120.	B
33.	A	77.	B	121.	D
34.	D	78.	C	122.	C
35.	A	79.	D	123.	D
36.	C	80.	B	124.	A
37.	D	81.	A	125.	B
38.	D	82.	B	126.	C
39.	A	83.	C	127.	D
40.	D	84.	D	128.	B
41.	A	85.	D	129.	A
42.	D	86.	D	130.	D
43.	B	87.	B		
44.	B	88.	B		

Rigor Table: Pre-test

	Easy %20	Average Rigor %40	Rigorous %40
Question #	2, 15, 16, 19, 21, 24, 29, 37, 48, 58, 62, 66, 68, 69, 72, 74, 79, 95, 96, 98, 101, 105, 106, 114, 119, 125, 128, 130	1, 8, 10, 11, 12, 17, 18, 20, 23, 25, 30, 31, 32, 34, 35, 38, 39, 40, 43, 44, 45, 46, 49, 52, 53, 59, 63, 64, 67, 70, 75, 77, 80, 82, 84, 86, 87, 91, 92, 93, 97, 99, 103, 107, 108, 111, 115, 116, 120, 122, 126, 127, 129	3, 4, 5, 6, 7, 9, 13, 14, 22, 26, 27, 28, 33, 36, 41, 42, 47, 50, 51, 54, 55, 56, 57, 60, 61, 65, 71, 73, 76, 78, 81, 83, 85, 88, 89, 90, 94, 100, 102, 104, 109, 110, 112, 113, 117, 118, 121, 123, 124

Rationales with Sample Questions: Pre Test

1. **A ruling pertaining to the use of evaluation procedures later consolidated in Public Law 94 – 142 resulted from which court case listed?**
   (Average Rigor) (Skill 1.1)

   A. Diana v. the State Board of Education (1970)
   B. Wyatt v. Stickney
   C. Larry P. v. Riles
   D. PASE v. Hannon

Answer: A. Diana v. the State Board of Education (1970)

Diana v. the State Board of Education resulted in the decision that all children must be evaluated in their native language.

2. **Included in data brought to the attention of Congress regarding the evaluation procedures for education of students with disabilities was the fact that:**
   (Easy) (Skill 1.1)

   A. There were a large number of children and youths with disabilities in the United States.
   B. Many children with disabilities were not receiving an appropriate education.
   C. Many parents of children with disabilities were forced to seek services outside of the public realm.
   D. All of the above

Answer: D. All of the above

All three factors, and many more, have driven Congress to act.

3. The Individuals with Disabilities Education Act (IDEA) was signed into law in and later reauthorized through a second revision in what years?
(Rigorous) (Skill 1.1)

   A. 1975 and 2004
   B. 1980 and 1990
   C. 1990 and 2004
   D. 1995 and 2001

Answer: C. 1990 and 2004

IDEA, Public Law 101-476, is a consolidation and reauthorization of all prior special education mandates, with amendments. It was signed into law by President Bush on October 30, 1990. Revision of IDEA occurred in 2004, and IDEA was re-authorized as the Individuals with Disabilities Education Improvement Act of 2004 (IDEIA 2004). IDEIA 2004 is commonly referred to as IDEA 2004 and was effective on July 1, 2005.

4. How was the training of special education teachers changed by the No Child Left Behind Act of 2002?
(Rigorous) (Skill 1.1)

   A. It required all special education teachers to be certified in reading and math.
   B. It required all special education teachers to take the same coursework as general education teachers.
   C. If a special education teacher is teaching a core subject, he or she must meet the standard of a highly-qualified teacher in that subject.
   D. All of the above

Answer: C. If a special education teacher is teaching a core subject, he or she must meet the standard of a highly-qualified teacher in that subject.

In order for special education teachers to be a student's sole teacher of a core subject, they must meet the professional criteria of NCLB. They must be *highly qualified*, that is certified or licensed in their area of special education, and show proof of a specific level of professional development in the core subjects that they teach. As special education teachers receive specific education in the core subject they teach, they will be better prepared to teach to the same level of learning standards as the general education teacher.

5. **The No Child Left Behind Act (NCLB) affected students with Limited English Proficiency (LEP) by:**
(Rigorous) (Skill 1.1)

   A. Requiring these students to demonstrate English Language Proficiency before a High School Diploma is granted.
   B. Providing allowances for schools not to require them to take and pass state Reading Exams (RCTs) if the students were enrolled in U.S. schools for less than a year.
   C. Providing allowances for these students to opt out of state math tests if the students were enrolled in a U.S. school for less than one year.
   D. Both B and C

Answer: A. Requiring these students to demonstrate English Language Proficiency before a High School Diploma is granted.

The No Child Left Behind Act (NCLB) requires these students to demonstrate English Language Proficiency before a High School Diploma is granted.

6. **Which of the following is a specific change of language in the IDEA?**
(Rigorous) (Skill 1.1)

   A. The term "Disorder" changed to "Disability."
   B. The term "Children" changed to "Children and Youth."
   C. The term "Handicapped" changed to "Impairments."
   D. The term "Handicapped" changed to "With Disabilities."

Answer: D. The term "Handicapped" changed to "With Disabilities."

"Children" became "individuals," highlighting the fact that some students with special needs were adolescents, not just "children". The word "handicapped" was changed to "with disabilities," denoting the difference between limitations imposed by society (handicap) and an inability to do certain things (disability). "With disabilities" also demonstrates that the person is thought of first, and the disabling condition is but one of the characteristics of the individual.

7. **Which component changed with the reauthorization of the Education for all Handicapped Children Act of 1975 (EHA) 1990 EHA Amendment?**
(Rigorous) (Skill 1.1)

   A. Specific terminology
   B. Due process protections
   C. Non-discriminatory reevaluation procedures
   D. Individual education plans

Answer: A. Specific terminology

See Skill 1.1 Question # 6.

8. **The definition of assistive technology devices was amended in the IDEA reauthorization of 2004 to exclude what?**
(Average Rigor) (Skill 1.1)

   A. iPods and other hand-held devices
   B. Computer enhanced technology
   C. Surgically implanted devices
   D. Braille and/or special learning aids

Answer: C. Surgically implanted devices

The definition of assistive technology devices was amended to exclude devices that are surgically implanted (i.e. cochlear implants) and clarified that students with assistive technology devices shall not be prevented from having special education services. Assistive technology devices may need to be monitored by school personnel, but schools are not responsible for the implantation or replacement of such devices surgically.

9. **Which is untrue about the Americans with disabilities Act (ADA)?**
   (Rigorous) (Skill 1.1)

   A. It was signed into law by President Bush the same year as IDEA.
   B. It reauthorized the discretionary programs of EHA.
   C. It gives protection to all people on the basis of race, sex, national origin, and religion.
   D. It guarantees equal opportunities to persons with disabilities in employment, public accommodations, transportation, government services, and telecommunications.

Answer: B It reauthorized the discretionary programs of EHA.

EHA is the precursor of IDEA, the Individuals with Disabilities Education Act. ADA, however, is Public Law 101 – 336, the Americans with disabilities Act, which gives civil rights protection to all individuals with disabilities in private sector employment, all public services, public accommodations, transportation and telecommunications. It was patterned after the Rehabilitation Act of 1973.

10. **The opportunity for persons with disabilities to live as close to the normal as possible describes:**
    (Average Rigor) (Skill 1.1)

    A. Least restrictive environment
    B. Normalization
    C. Mainstreaming
    D. Deinstitutionalization

Answer: B. Normalization

The other terms listed all refer to specific types of opportunities for normalization for persons with disabilities.

11. Requirements for evaluations were changed in IDEA 2004 to reflect that no 'single' assessment or measurement tool can be used to determine special education qualification, furthering that there was a disproportionate representation of what types of students?
(Average Rigor) (Skill 1.1)

   A. Disabled
   B. Foreign
   C. Gifted
   D. Minority and bilingual

Answer: D. Minority and bilingual

IDEA 2004 recognized that there exists a disproportionate representation of minorities and bilingual students and that pre-service interventions that are *scientifically based on early reading programs, positive behavioral interventions and support,* and early intervening services may prevent some of those children from needing special education services. In addition, it recognized that students whose native language is not English do not have a language disability. They simply need to learn English.

12. What determines whether a person is entitled to protection under Section 504?
(Average Rigor) (Skill 1.1)

   A. The individual must meet the definition of a person with a disability.
   B. The person must be able to meet the requirements of a particular program in spite of his or her disability.
   C. The school, business, or other facility must be the recipient of federal funding assistance.
   D. All of the above

Answer: D. All of the above

To be entitled to protection under Section 504, an individual must meet the definition of a person with a disability, which is: any person who (i) has a physical or mental impairment which substantially limits one or more of that person's major life activities, (ii) has a record of such impairment, or (iii) is regarded as having such an impairment. Major life activities are: caring for oneself, performing manual tasks, walking, seeing, hearing, speaking, breathing, learning, and working. The person must also be "otherwise qualified," which means that the person must be able to meet the requirements of a particular program in spite of the disability. The person must also be afforded "reasonable accommodations" by recipients of federal financial assistance.

13. **Legislation in Public Law 94 – 142 attempts to:**
    (Rigorous) (Skill 1.1)

    A. Match the child's educational needs with appropriate educational services.
    B. Include parents in the decisions made about their child's education.
    C. Establish a means by which parents can provide input.
    D. All of the above

Answer: D All of the above

Much of what was stated in separate court rulings and mandated legislation was brought together into what is now considered to be the "backbone" of special education. Public Law 94 – 142 (Education for All Handicapped Children Act) was signed into law by President Ford in 1975. It was the culmination of a great deal of litigation and legislation from the late 1960's to the mid 1970's that included decisions supporting the need to assure an appropriate education to all persons regardless of race, creed, or disability. In 1990, this law was reauthorized and renamed the Individuals with Disabilities Education Act, IDEA.

14. **Effective transition was included in:**
    (Rigorous) (Skill 1.1)

    A. President Bush's 1990 State of the Union Message
    B. Public Law 101-476
    C. Public Law 95-207
    D. Both A and B

Answer: D. Both A and B

With the enactment of P. L. 101-476 (IDEA), transition services became a right.

15. **The Free Appropriate Public Education (FAPE) describes Special Education and related services as?**
(Easy) (Skill 1.2)

   A. Public expenditure and standard to the state educational agency.
   B. Provided in conformity with each student's individualized education program, if the program is developed to meet requirements of the law.
   C. Including preschool, elementary, and/or secondary education in the state involved.
   D. All of the above

Answer: D. All of the above

FAPE states that special education and related services are provided at public expense; meet the standards of the state educational agency; include preschool, elementary, and/or secondary education in the state involved; and are provided in conformity with each student's IEP if the program is developed to meet requirements of the law.

16. **Jane is a third grader. Mrs. Smith, her teacher, noted that Jane was having difficulty with math and reading assignments. The results from recent diagnostic tests showed a strong sight vocabulary and strength in computational skills, but a weakness in comprehending what she read. This weakness was apparent in mathematical word problems as well. The multi-disciplinary team recommended placement in a special education resource room for learning disabilities two periods each school day. For the remainder of the school day, her placement will be:**
(Easy) (Skill 1.2)

   A. In the regular classroom
   B. At a special school
   C. In a self-contained classroom
   D. In a resource room for mental retardation

Answer: A. In the regular classroom

The resource room is a special room inside the school environment where the child goes to be taught by a teacher who is certified in the area of disability. We hope the accommodations and services provided in the resource room will help her to catch up and perform with her peers in the regular classroom.

17. Which of the following must be provided in a written notice to parents when proposing a child's educational placement?
(Average Rigor) (Skill 1.2)

   A. A list of parental due process safeguards
   B. A list of current test scores
   C. A list of persons responsible for the child's education
   D. A list of academic subjects the child has passed

Answer: A. A list of parental due process safeguards

Written notice must be provided to parents prior to a proposal or refusal to initiate or make a change in the child's identification, evaluation, or educational placement. Notices must contain:
- A listing of parental due process safeguards
- A description and a rationale for the chosen action
- A detailed listing of components (e.g., tests, records, reports) that were the basis for the decision
- Assurance that the language and content of the notices were understood by the parents

18. Zero Reject requires all children with disabilities be provided with what?
(Average Rigor) (Skill 1.2)

   A. Total exclusion of functional exclusion
   B. Adherence to the annual local education agency (LEA) reporting
   C. Free, appropriate public education
   D. Both B and C

Answer: C. Free, appropriate public education

The principle of zero reject requires that all children with disabilities be provided with a free, appropriate public education, and the LEA reporting procedure locates, identifies, and evaluates children with disabilities within a given jurisdiction to ensure their attendance in public school.

19. Students who receive special services in a regular classroom with consultation generally have academic and/or social-interpersonal performance deficits at which level of severity?
    (Easy) (Skill 1.2)

    A. Mild
    B. Moderate
    C. Severe
    D. Profound

Answer: A. Mild

The majority of students receiving special services are enrolled primarily in regular classes. Those with mild learning and behavior problems exhibit academic and/or social interpersonal deficits that are often evident only in a school-related setting. These students appear no different to their peers, physically.

20. The greatest number of students receiving special services is enrolled primarily in:
    (Average Rigor) (Skill 1.2)

    A. The regular classroom
    B. The resource room
    C. Self-contained classrooms
    D. Special schools

Answer: A. The regular classroom

See previous question.

21. **The most restrictive environment in which an individual might be placed and receive instruction is that of:**
(Easy) (Skill 1.2)

   A. Institutional setting
   B. Homebound instruction
   C. Special schools
   D. Self-contained special classes

Answer: A. Institutional setting

Individuals who require significantly modified environments for care treatment and accommodation are usually educated in an institutional setting. They usually have profound/multiple disorders.

22. **The law affects required components of the IEP; elements required by the IEP and the law are:**
(Rigorous) (Skill 1.3)

   A. Present level of academic and functional performance; statement of how the disability affects the student's involvement and progress; evaluation criteria and timeliness for instructional objective achievement; modifications of accommodations
   B. Projected dates for services initiation with anticipated frequency, location and duration; statement of when parent will be notified; statement of annual goals
   C. Extent to which child will not participate in regular education program; transitional needs for students age 14.
   D. All of the above.

Answer: D. All of the above

IEPs outline very specific elements that are required, and you may review them in Skill 1.3 under IEP. Educators must keep themselves apprised of the changes and amendments to laws, such as IDEA 2004, with addendums released in October of 2006.

23. **IEPs continue to have multiple sections; one section, present levels, now addresses what?**
(Average Rigor) (Skill 1.3)

   A. Academic achievement and functional performance
   B. English as a second language
   C. Functional performance
   D. Academic achievement

Answer: A. Academic achievement and functional performance

Individualized Education Plans (IEPS) continue to have multiple sections. One section, present levels, now addresses academic achievement and functional performance. Annual IEP goals must now address the same areas.

24. **What is true about IDEA? In order to be eligible, a student must:**
(Easy) (Skill 1.4)

   A. Have a medical disability
   B. Have a disability that fits into one of the categories listed in the law
   C. Attend a private school
   D. Be a slow learner

Answer: B. Have a disability that fits into one of the categories listed in the law

IDEA is a legal instrument; thus, it is defined by law. Every aspect in the operation of IDEA is laid out in law.

25. **Changes in requirements for Current Levels of performance require:?** *(Average Rigor) (Skill 1.4)*

   A. student voice in each Present Level of Performance.
   B. CSE chair must tell parents when child has unrealistic goals.
   C. Parent/Guardian must attend either by phone conference or in person.
   D. Teachers must write post adult outcomes assigning a student to a specific field.

Answer: A. student voice in each Present Level of Performance

Idea's new Indicator 13 is changing the way IEPs are written. The federal government is requiring changes in IEPs to create an easier way to collect statistics on student success at reaching post school goals. While many of the requirements have been used for years, compliance is now being measured by the items listed below.

Present Levels of Performance: Student voice must be included in each Present Level of Performance. This means that Academic, Social, Physical, Management, etc. must include one student voice statement either in the strengths or needs or both. For example, "John reads fluently on a 3rd grade level. He is able to add and subtract two digit numbers. He has difficulty with grouping and multiplying. *John states that he would rather read than do math."* Student voice can express either his/her strengths, preferences and/or interests. When the child begins to do vocational assessments, student voice should be related to transition to post-school activities of his/her choice. In addition, Present Levels of Performance must indicate why a student's post adult goals are realistic, or why they are not.

26. **Developmental Disabilities:**
   (Rigorous) (Skill 1.4)

   A. Is the categorical name for mental retardation in IDEA
   B. Includes congenital conditions, such as severe Spina Bifida, deafness, blindness, or profound mental retardation
   C. Includes children who contract diseases, such as polio or meningitis, and who are left in an incapacitated functional state
   D. Both B and C

Answer: D. Both B and C

Developmental disabilities include congenital conditions and children who contract diseases and are left in an incapacitated functional state.

27. Which of the following goals reflects new IDEA requirements?
(Rigorous) (Skill 1.3)

A. Janet wants to be a doctor.
B. Frank intends to go to The Culinary Institute.
C. Janet will go to college.
D. Carmel currently lives independently on her own.

Answer: C. Janet will go to college.
Post adult outcome must now be written with a "student will" statement.

28. The definition for "Other Health Impaired (OHI)" in IDEA:
(Rigorous) (Skill 1.4)

A. Is the definition that accepts heart conditions
B. Includes deafness, blindness, or profound mental retardation
C. Includes Autism and PDD
D. Includes cochlear implants

Answer: A. Is the definition that accepts heart conditions

This is the definition that accepts heart conditions. OHI includes a variety of reasons and diagnoses, including heart conditions.

29. Which is an educational characteristic common to students with mild intellectual learning and behavioral disabilities?
(Easy) (Skill 1.5)

A. Show interest in schoolwork
B. Have intact listening skills
C. Require modification in classroom instruction
D. Respond better to passive than to active learning tasks

Answer: C. Require modification in classroom instruction

Some of the characteristics of students with mild learning and behavioral disabilities are as follows: Lack of interest in schoolwork; prefer concrete rather than abstract lessons; weak listening skills; low achievement; limited verbal and/or writing skills; respond better to active rather than passive learning tasks; have areas of talent or ability often overlooked by teachers; prefer to receive special help in regular classroom; higher dropout rate than regular education students; achieve in accordance with teacher expectations; require modification in classroom instruction; and are easily distracted.

30. **In general, characteristics of students with learning disabilities include:**
 (Average Rigor) (Skill 1.5)

    A. A low level of performance in a majority of academic skill areas
    B. Limited cognitive ability
    C. A discrepancy between achievement and potential
    D. A uniform pattern of academic development

Answer: C A discrepancy between achievement and potential

The individual with a specific learning disability exhibits a discrepancy between achievement and potential.

31. **Michael's teacher complains that he is constantly out of his seat. She also reports that he has trouble paying attention to what is going on in class for more than a couple of minutes at a time. He appears to be trying, but his writing is often illegible, containing many reversals. Although he seems to want to please, he is very impulsive and stays in trouble with his teacher. He is failing reading, and his math grades, though somewhat better, are still below average. Michael's psychometric evaluation should include assessment for:**
 (Average Rigor)(Skill 1.5)

    A. Mild mental retardation
    B. Specific learning disabilities
    C. Mild behavior disorders
    D. Hearing impairment

Answer: B Specific learning disabilities

Some of the characteristics of persons with learning disabilities are:
- Hyperactivity: a rate of motor activity higher than normal
- Perceptual difficulties: visual, auditory, and haptic perceptual problems
- Perceptual-motor impairments: poor integration of visual and motor systems, often affecting fine motor coordination
- Disorders of memory and thinking: memory deficits, trouble with problem-solving, concept formation and association, poor awareness of own metacognitive skills (learning strategies)
- Impulsiveness: acts before considering consequences, poor impulse control, often followed by remorselessness
- Academic problems in reading, math, writing or spelling; significant discrepancies in ability levels

32. **Joey is in a mainstreamed preschool program. One of the means his teacher uses in determining growth in adaptive skills is that of observation. Some questions about Joey's behavior that she might ask include:**
(Average Rigor) (Skill 1.5)

   A. Is he able to hold a cup?
   B. Can he call the name of any of his toys?
   C. Can he reach for an object and grasp it?
   D. All of the above

Answer: D. All of the above

Here are some characteristics of individuals with mental retardation or intellectual disabilities:
- IQ of 70 or below
- Limited cognitive ability; delayed academic achievement, particularly in language-related subjects
- Deficits in memory, which often relate to poor initial perception, or inability to apply stored information to relevant situations
- Impaired formulation of learning strategies
- Difficulty in attending to relevant aspects of stimuli: slowness in reaction time or in employing alternate strategies
- Deficits in many adaptive behavior skills

33. **Individuals with mental retardation can be characterized as:**
(Rigorous) (Skill 1.5)

   A. Often indistinguishable from normal developing children at an early age
   B. Having a higher than normal rate of motor activity
   C. Displaying significant discrepancies in ability levels
   D. Uneducable in academic skills

Answer: A. Often indistinguishable from normal developing children at an early age

See rationale for question 32 for some characteristics of individuals with mental retardation or intellectual disabilities.

34. **Which of the following statements about children with an emotional/behavioral disorder is true?**
    (Average Rigor) (Skill 1.5)

    A. They have very high IQs.
    B. They display poor social skills.
    C. They are poor academic achievers.
    D. Both B and C

Answer: D. Both B and C

Children who exhibit mild behavioral disorders are characterized by:
- Average or above average scores on intelligence tests
- Poor academic achievement; learned helplessness
- Unsatisfactory interpersonal relationships
- Immaturity; attention seeking
- Aggressive, acting-out behavior: (hitting, fighting, teasing, yelling, refusing to comply with requests, excessive attention seeking, poor anger control, temper tantrums, hostile reactions, defiant use of language) OR Anxious, withdrawn behavior: (infantile behavior, social isolation, few friends, withdrawal into fantasy, fears, hypochondria, unhappiness, crying)

35. **Which behavior would be expected at the mild level of emotional/behavioral disorders?**
    (Average Rigor) (Skill 1.5)

    A. Attention seeking
    B. Inappropriate affect
    C. Self-Injurious
    D. Poor sense of identity

Answer: A. Attention seeking

See rationale to question 34.

36. **Which of the following is true about autism?**
    (Rigorous) (Skill 1.5)

    A. It is caused by having cold, aloof, or hostile parents.
    B. Approximately 4 out of 10 people have autism.
    C. It is a separate exceptionality category in IDEA.
    D. It is a form of mental illness.

Answer: C. It is a separate exceptionality category in IDEA.

In IDEA, the 1990 Amendment to the Education for All Handicapped Children Act, autism was classified as a separate exceptionality category. It is thought to be caused by a neurological or biochemical dysfunction. It generally becomes evident before age 3. The condition occurs in about 4 of every 10,000 persons. Smith and Luckasson, 1992, describe it as a severe language disorder that affects thinking, communication, and behavior. They list the following characteristics:

- **Absent or distorted relationships with people**—inability to relate with people except as objects, inability to express affection, or ability to build and maintain only distant, suspicious, or bizarre relationships.
- **Extreme or peculiar problems in communication**—absence of verbal language or language that is not functional, such as echolalia (parroting what one hears), misuse of pronouns (e.g., he for you or I for her), neologisms (made-up meaningless words or sentences), talk that bears little or no resemblance to reality.
- **Self-stimulation**—repetitive stereotyped behavior that seems to have no purposes other than providing sensory stimulation. This may take a wide variety of forms, such as swishing saliva, twirling objects, patting one's cheeks, flapping one's arms, staring, etc.
- **Self-injury**—repeated physical self-abuse, such as biting, scratching, or poking oneself, head banging, etc.
- **Perceptual anomalies**—unusual responses or absence of response to stimuli that seem to indicate sensory impairment or unusual sensitivity.

37. **Autism is a condition characterized by:**
    (Easy) (Skill 1.5)

    A. Distorted relationships with others
    B. Perceptual anomalies
    C. Self-stimulation
    D. All of the above

Answer: D. All of the above

See previous question.

38. **As a separate exceptionality category in IDEA, autism:**
    (Average Rigor) (Skill 1.5)

    A. Includes emotional/behavioral disorders as defined in federal regulations
    B. Adversely affects educational performance
    C. Is thought to be a form of mental illness
    D. Is a developmental disability that affects verbal and non-verbal communication

Answer: D. Is a developmental disability that affects verbal and non-verbal communication

See rationale to question 36.

39. **Normality in child behavior is influenced by society's:**
    (Average Rigor) (Skill 1.5)

    A. Attitudes and cultural beliefs
    B. Hereditary factors
    C. Prenatal care
    D. Attitudes and Victorian era motto

Answer: A. Attitudes and cultural beliefs

Society's attitudes and cultural beliefs influence normality and the perception of normality in child behavior.

40. **The CST coordinates and participates in due diligence through what process?**
    (Average Rigor) (Skill 1.6)

    A. Child study team meets for the first time without parents.
    B. Teachers take child learning concerns to the school counselor.
    C. School counselor contacts parents for permission to perform screening assessments.
    D. All of the above

Answer: D. All of the above

The CST coordinates and participates in due diligence through a process that includes teachers' or parents' concerns about academic or functional development and goes to the counselor who then obtains permission for screening assessments of child's skills, and the results determine need. If needed, the child study team meets without parents first.

41. Which of the following examples would be considered of highest priority when determining the need for the delivery of appropriate special education and related services?
(Rigorous) (Skill 1.6)

- A. An eight-year-old boy is repeating first grade for the second time and exhibits problems with toileting, gross motor functions, and remembering number and letter symbols. His regular classroom teacher claims the referral forms are too time-consuming and refuses to complete them. He also refuses to make accommodations because he feels every child should be treated alike.
- B. A six-year-old girl who has been diagnosed as autistic is placed in a special education class within the local school. Her mother wants her to attend residential school next year even though the girl is showing progress.
- C. A ten-year-old girl with profound mental retardation who is receiving education services in a state institution.
- D. A twelve-year-old boy with mild disabilities who was placed in a behavior disorders program but displays obvious perceptual deficits (e.g., reversal of letters and symbols and inability to discriminate sounds). He originally was thought to have a learning disability but did not meet state criteria for this exceptionality category based on results of standard scores. He has always had problems with attending to a task and is now beginning to get into trouble during seatwork time. His teacher feels that he will eventually become a real behavior problem. He receives social skills training in the resource room one period a day.

Answer: A. An eight-year-old boy is repeating first grade for the second time and exhibits problems with toileting, gross motor functions, and remembering number and letter symbols. His regular classroom teacher claims the referral forms are too time-consuming and refuses to complete them. He also refuses to make accommodations because he feels every child should be treated alike.

No modifications are being made, so the child is not receiving any services whatsoever. Note also, that the teacher in this scenario is in violation of the law.

42. When a student is identified as being at-risk academically or socially what does Federal law hope for first?
(Rigorous) (Skill 1.6)

   A. Move the child quickly to assessment.
   B. Place the child in special education as soon as possible.
   C. Observe the child to determine what is wrong.
   D. Perform remedial intervention in the classroom.

Answer: D. Perform remedial intervention in the classroom.

Once a student is identified as being at-risk academically or socially, remedial interventions are attempted within the regular classroom. Federal legislation requires that sincere efforts be made to help the child learn in the regular classroom.

43. What do the 9th and 10th Amendments to the U.S. Constitution state about education?
(Average Rigor) (Skill 1.8)

   A. That education belongs to the people
   B. That education is an unstated power vested in the states
   C. That elected officials mandate education
   D. That education is free

Answer: B. That education is an unstated power vested in the states

The 9th and 10th Amendments state that education is an unstated power vested in the states.

44. The IDEA states that child assessment is?
(Average Rigor) (Skill 2.1)

   A. At intervals with teacher discretion
   B. Continuous on a regular basis
   C. Left to the counselor
   D. Conducted annually

Answer: B. Continuous on a regular basis

Assessments in Special Education are continuous and occur on a regular basis.

45. **Safeguards against bias and discrimination in the assessment of children include:**
(Average Rigor) (Skill 2.2)

   A. The testing of a child in Standard English
   B. The requirement for the use of one standardized test
   C. The use of evaluative materials in the child's native language or other mode of communication
   D. All testing performed by a certified, licensed psychologist

Answer: C. The use of evaluative materials in the child's native language or other mode of communication

The law requires that the child be evaluated in his native language or mode of communication. The idea that a licensed psychologist evaluates the child does not meet the criteria if it is not done in the child's normal mode of communication.

46. **Which is characteristic of group tests?**
(Average Rigor) (Skill 2.3)

   A. Directions are always read to students.
   B. The examiner monitors several students at the same time.
   C. The teacher must follow a standardized procedure.
   D. Diagnostic information cannot be gathered.

Answer: B. The examiner monitors several students at the same time.

The group test variable simply refers to the manner of presentation of the test. A group test is given to more than one student at a time and the teacher monitors all the students taking the test simultaneously. Group assessments can be formal or informal, standardized or not, criterion or norm referenced. Individual assessments can be found in all these types, as well.

47. **For which of the following uses are standardized individual tests MOST appropriate?**
    (Rigorous) (Skill 2.3)

    A. Screening students to determine possible need for special education services
    B. Evaluation of special education curricula
    C. Tracking of gifted students
    D. Evaluation of a student for eligibility and placement, or individualized program planning, in special education

Answer: D. Evaluation of a student for eligibility and placement, or individualized program planning, in special education

See previous question. Standardized tests are useful for these decisions, because they are very objective and can provide a wide range of data, from comparison with grade peers (a norm-referenced test), to mastery of certain skills (criterion referenced test), to pinpointing specific areas of strength or weakness (intelligence tests or psychological tests).

48. **Which of the following is an advantage of giving informal, individual rather than standardized group tests?**
    (Easy) (Skill 2.3)

    A. Questions can be modified to reveal a specific student's strategies or misconceptions..
    B. The test administrator can clarify or rephrase questions.
    C. They can be inserted into the class quickly on an as needed basis.
    D. All of the above

Answer: D. All of the above
Standardized group tests are administered to a group in a specifically prescribed manner, with strict rules to keep procedures, scoring, and interpretation of results uniform in all cases. Such tests allow comparisons to be made across populations, ages or grades. *Informal* assessments have less objective measures, and may include anecdotes or observations that may or may not be quantified, interviews, informal questioning during a task, etc. An example of an informal *individually* administered assessment might be watching a student sort objects to see what attribute is most important to the student, or questioning a student to see what he or she found confusing about a task. All of the answers listed are advantages of giving informal individual rather than standardized group tests. Since standardized tests require rigid adherence to a precise format and presentation, they do not have the flexibility needed to modify questions to follow an individual student's strategies or needs as they work.

49. Mrs. Stokes has been teaching her third grade students about mammals during a recent science unit. Which of the following would be true of a criterion-referenced test she might administer at the conclusion of the unit?
(Average Rigor) (Skill 2.3)

   A. It will be based on unit objectives.
   B. Derived scores will be used to rank student achievement.
   C. Standardized scores are effective of national performance samples.
   D. All of the above

Answer: A. It will be based on unit objectives.

Criterion-referenced tests measure the progress made by individuals in mastering specific skills. The content is based on a specific set of objectives rather than on the general curriculum. Criterion-referenced tests provide measurements pertaining to the information a given student needs to know and the skills that student needs to master.

50. For which of the following purposes is a norm-referenced test LEAST appropriate?
(Rigorous) (Skill 2.3)

   A. Screening
   B. Individual program planning
   C. Program evaluation
   D. Making placement decisions

Answer: B. Individual program planning

Norm-referenced tests provide a means of comparing a student's performance to the performance typically expected of others the same age or grade but should not be used for individual program planning. Norm-referenced tests have a large advantage over criterion-referenced tests when used for screening or program evaluation. Norm-referenced tests provide a means of comparing a student's performance to the performance typically expected of others of his age or grade

51. Criterion-referenced tests can provide information about: *(Rigorous) (Skill 2.3)*

    A. Whether a student has mastered prerequisite skills
    B. Whether a student is ready to proceed to the next level of instruction
    C. Which instructional materials might be helpful in covering program objectives
    D. All of the above

Answer: A. Whether a student has mastered prerequisite skills

In criterion-referenced testing, the emphasis is on assessing specific and relevant behaviors that have been mastered. Items on criterion-referenced tests are often linked directly to specific instructional objectives.

52. Which of the following purposes of testing calls for an informal test? *(Average Rigor) (Skill 2.3)*

    A. Screening a group of children to determine their readiness for the first reader.
    B. Analyzing the responses of a student with a disability to various presentations of content material to see which strategy works for him.
    C. Evaluating the effectiveness of a fourth grade math program at the end of its first year of use in a specific school..
    D. Determining the general level of intellectual functioning of a class of fifth graders.

Answer: B. Analyzing the responses of a student with a disability to various presentations of content material to see which strategy works for him.

Formal tests, such as standardized tests or textbook quizzes are objective tests that include primarily questions for which there is only one correct answer. Some are teacher prepared, but many are commercially prepared and frequently standardized. To analyze the response of a student to different types of instructional presentation informal methods such as observation and questioning are more useful.

53. **Which of the following is not a true statement about informal tests? (Average Rigor) (Skill 2.3)**

   A. Informal tests are useful in comparing students to others of their age or grade level.
   B. The correlation between curriculum and test criteria is much higher in informal tests.
   C. Informal tests are useful in evaluating n individual's response to instruction.
   D. Informal tests are used to diagnose a student's particular strengths and weaknesses for purpose of planning individual programs.

Answer: A. Informal tests are useful in comparing students to others of their age or grade..

Informal tests do NOT allow comparison among students of the same age or grade. Norm referenced tests are standardized tests that compare a student's responses to those of a large population of the same age or grade. Informal tests are not useful in comparing students to others in the population because they are neither standardized nor normed. Informal tests are often teacher made and usually criterion referenced. They are useful for a variety of diagnostic and instructional planning purposes.

54. **For which situation might a teacher be apt to select a formal test? (Rigorous) (Skill 2.3)**

   A. A pretest for studying world religions
   B. A weekly spelling test
   C. To compare student progress with that of peers of same age or grade level on a national basis
   D. To determine which content objectives outlined on the student's IEP were mastered

Answer: C. To compare student progress with that of peers of same age or grade level on a national basis

See previous question.

55. The Key Math Diagnostic Arithmetic Test is an individually administered test of math skills. It is comprised of fourteen subtests, which are classified into the major math areas of content, operations, and applications for which subtest scores are reported. The test manual describes the population sample upon which the test was normed and reports data pertaining to reliability and validity. In addition, for each item in the test, a behavioral objective is presented. From the description, it can be determined that this achievement test is:
(Rigorous) (Skill 2.3)

   A. Individually administered
   B. Criterion-referenced
   C. Diagnostic
   D. All of the above

Answer: D. All of the above

The test has a limited content designed to measure to what extent the student has mastered specific areas in math. The expressions "individually administered" and "diagnostic" appear in the description of the test.

56. The best measures of a student's functional capabilities and entry-level skills are:
(Rigorous) (Skill 2.3)

   A. Norm-referenced tests
   B. Teacher-made post-tests
   C. Standardized IQ tests
   D. Criterion-referenced measures

Answer: D. Criterion-referenced measures

Criterion-referenced measures are useful for assessment of a student's functional capabilities and entry-level skills. Unlike norm-referenced tests, which compare an individual with others of the same grade or age level, criterion-referenced tests, measure the level of functions and skills of the individual.

57. One of your students receives a percentile rank of 45 on a standardized test. This indicates that the student's score: *(Rigorous) (Skill 2.4)*

    A. Consisted of 45 correct answers
    B. Was at the point above which 45% of the other scores fell
    C. Was at the point below which 45% of the other scores fell
    D. Was below passing

Answer: C. Was at the point below which 45% of the other scores fell

Percentile scores indicate how well the student did compared to the other students tested. A percentile rank of 45 indicates that the student's score was at the point below which 45% of the other scores fell.

58. Children who write poorly might be given tests that allow oral responses, that is unless the purpose for giving the test is to: *(Easy) (Skill 2.5)*

    A. Assess handwriting skills
    B. Test for organization of thoughts
    C. Answer questions pertaining to math reasoning
    D. Assess rote memory

Answer: A. Assess handwriting skills

It is necessary to have the child write if we are assessing his skill in that domain.

59. Alternative assessments include all of the following EXCEPT: *(Average Rigor) (Skill 2.5)*

    A. Portfolios
    B. Interviews
    C. Textbook chapter tests
    D. Student choice of assessment format

Answer: C. Textbook chapter tests

Textbook chapter tests are formal, usually multiple choice tests with one fixed, correct answer. Portfolios, interviews and student choices in assessment format are alternative assessments with flexible formats and alternative, individually based, criteria.

60. Which of the following is an example of an alternative assessment?
    (Rigorous) (Skill 2.5)

    A. Testing skills in a "real world" setting in several settings
    B. Pre-test of student knowledge of fractions before beginning wood shop
    C. Answering an essay question that allows for creative thought
    D. A compilation of a series of tests in a portfolio

Answer: A. Testing skills in a "real world" setting in several settings

Naturalistic assessment is a form of alternative assessment that requires testing in actual application settings of life skills. The skill of using money correctly could be correctly assessed in this method by taking the student shopping in different settings.

61. Acculturation refers to the individual's:
    (Rigorous) (Skill 2.6)

    A. Gender
    B. Experiential background
    C. Social class
    D. Ethnic background

Answer: B. Experiential background

A person's culture has little to do with gender, social class, or ethnicity. A person is the product of his experiences. Acculturation is defined as: differences in experiential background.

62. To which aspect does fair assessment relate?
    (Easy) (Skill 2.6)

    A. Representation
    B. Acculturation
    C. Language
    D. All of the above

Answer: D. All of the above

All three aspects are necessary and vital for assessment to be fair.

63. A test that measures students' skill development in academic content areas is classified as an _____ test.
(Average Rigor) (Skill 3.1)

   A. Achievement
   B. Aptitude
   C. Adaptive
   D. Intelligence

Answer: A. Achievement

Achievement tests directly assess students' skill development in academic content areas. They measure the degree to which a student has benefited from education and/or life experiences compared to others of the same age or grade level. They may be used as diagnostic tests to find strengths and weaknesses of students. They may also be used for screening, placement, progress evaluation, and curricular effectiveness.

64. Which of the following is an example of tactile perception?
(Average Rigor) (Skill 3.2)

   A. Making an angel in the snow with one's body
   B. Running a specified course
   C. Identifying a rough surface with eyes closed
   D. Demonstrating aerobic exercises

Answer: C. Identifying a rough surface with eyes closed

Tactile means having to do with touch.

65. Which of the following activities best exemplifies a kinesthetic exercise in developing body awareness?
(Rigorous) (Skill 3.2)

   A. Touching materials of different textures
   B. Playing a song and movement game like "Looby Loo"
   C. Identifying geometric shapes being drawn on one's back
   D. Making a shadow-box project

Answer: B. Playing a game like "Looby Loo"

Kinesthetic means having to do with body movement.

66. Which of the following teaching activities is LEAST likely to enhance observational learning in students with special needs?
(Easy) (Skill 3.2)

   A. A verbal description of the task to be performed, followed by having the children immediately attempt to perform the instructed behavior
   B. A demonstration of the behavior, followed by an immediate opportunity for the children to imitate the behavior
   C. A simultaneous demonstration and explanation of the behavior, followed by ample opportunity for the children to rehearse the instructed behavior
   D. Physically guiding the children through the behavior to be imitated, while verbally explaining the behavior

Answer: A. A verbal description of the task to be performed, followed by having the children immediately attempt to perform the instructed behavior

Students are given verbal instructions only. The children are not given a chance to observe or see the behavior so that they can imitate it. Some of the students may have hearing deficiencies. Others may need visual or kinesthetic cues to help them understand what is wanted of them.

67. The _____ modality is most frequently used in the learning process.
(Average Rigor) (Skill 3.2)

   A. Auditory
   B. Visual
   C. Tactile
   D. All of the Above

Answer: D. All of the above

The auditory, visual, and tactile modalities are the ones frequently used in the learning process. We learn through an integration of these modalities (multi-sensory approach).

68. _____ is a method used to increase student engaged learning time by having students teach other students.
    (Easy) (Skill 3.2)

    A. Collaborative learning
    B. Engaged learning time
    C. Allocated learning time
    D. Teacher consultation

Answer: A. Collaborative learning

Collaborative learning is a method for increasing student learning time by having students teach other students.

69. Some environmental elements that influence the effectiveness of learning styles include all EXCEPT:
    (Easy) (Skill 3.2)

    A. Light
    B. Temperature
    C. Design
    D. Motivation

Answer: D. Motivation

Individual learning styles are influenced by environmental, emotional, sociological, and physical elements. Environmental elements include sound, light, temperature, and design. Emotional elements include motivation, persistence, responsibility, and structure. Motivation is not an environmental element.

70. In order for a student to function independently in the learning environment, which of the following must be true?
    (Average Rigor) (Skill 3.2)

    A. The learner must understand the nature of the content.
    B. The student must be able to do the assigned task.
    C. The teacher must communicate performance criteria to the learner.
    D. All of the above

Answer: D. All of the above

Together with the above, the child must be able to ask for and obtain assistance if necessary.

71. What can a teacher plan that will allow him/her to avoid adverse situations with students?
    (Rigorous) (Skill 3.2)

    A. Instructional techniques
    B. Instructional materials and formats
    C. Physical setting and environment
    D. All of the above

Answer: D. All of the above

It is the teacher's responsibility to select instructional practices that reflect students' individual learning needs and to incorporate a wide range of learning strategies and specialized materials to meet those needs. Students display preferences for certain learning styles, and these differences are also factors in the teacher's choice of presentation and materials. Physical settings, instructional arrangements, materials available, and presentation techniques, are all factors under the teacher's control and can be manipulated to meet student needs.

72. John learns best through the auditory channel, so his teacher wants to reinforce his listening skills. Through which of the following types of equipment would instruction be most effectively presented?
    (Easy) (Skill 3.2)

    A. Overhead projector
    B. Cassette player
    C. Microcomputer
    D. Opaque projector

Answer: B. Cassette player

An audio cassette player would help sharpen and further develop his listening skills, as he is an auditory learner.

73. **When teaching a student who is predominantly auditory to read, it is best to:**
    (Rigorous) (Skill 3.2)

    A. Stress sight vocabulary
    B. Stress phonetic analysis
    C. Stress the shape and configuration of the word
    D. Stress rapid reading

Answer: B. Stress the phonetic analysis

Sensory modalities are one of the physical elements that affect learning style. Some students learn best through their visual sense (sight), others through their auditory sense (hearing), and still others by doing, touching, and moving (tactile-kinesthetic). Auditory learners generally listen to people, follow verbal directions, and enjoy hearing records, cassette tapes, and stories. Phonics has to do with sound, an auditory stimulus. Since phonics involves attaching sounds to letters, visual stimuli, the child will need to integrate the two modalities. An auditory learner will start with the sounds, then move to visual cues.

74. **If a student is predominantly a visual learner, he may learn more effectively by:**
    (Easy) (Skill 3.2)

    A. Reading aloud while studying
    B. Listening to a cassette tape
    C. Watching a filmstrip
    D. Using body movement

Answer: C. Watching a filmstrip

Visual learners use their sense of sight, which is the sense being used to watch a filmstrip.

75. A prerequisite skill is:
(Average Rigor) (Skill 3.3)

A. The lowest order skill in a hierarchy of skills needed to perform a specific task
B. A skill that must be demonstrated before instruction on a specific task can begin
C. A tool for accomplishing task analysis
D. The smallest component of any skill

Answer: B. A skill that must be demonstrated before instruction on a specific task can begin

This is an enabling skill that a student needs in order to perform an objective successfully.

76. Presentation of tasks can be altered to match the student's rate of learning by:
(Rigorous) (Skill 3.3)

A. Describing how much of a topic is presented in one day and how much practice is assigned according to the student's abilities and learning style
B. Using task analysis, assign a certain number of skills to be mastered in a specific amount of time
C. Introducing a new task only when the student has demonstrated mastery of the previous task in the learning hierarchy
D. Both A and C

Answer: D. Both A and C

Pacing is the term used for altering of tasks to match the student's rate of learning. This can be done in two ways: altering the subject content and the rate at which tasks are presented.

77. All of the following are suggestions for altering the presentation of tasks to match the student's rate of learning EXCEPT:
(Average Rigor) (Skill 3.3)

   A. Teach in several shorter segments of time rather than a single lengthy session.
   B. Continue to teach a task until the lesson is completed in order to provide more time on task.
   C. Watch for nonverbal cues that indicate students are becoming confused, bored, or restless.
   D. Avoid giving students an inappropriate amount of written work.

Answer: B. Continue to teach a task until the lesson is completed in order to provide more time on task.

This action taken does not alter the subject content; neither does it alter the rate at which tasks are presented.

78. Which of the following is a good example of a generalization?
(Rigorous) (Skill 3.3)

   A. Jim has learned to add and is now ready to subtract.
   B. Sarah adds sets of units to obtain a product.
   C. Bill recognizes a vocabulary word on a billboard when traveling.
   D. Jane can spell the word "net" backwards to get the word "ten."

Answer: C. Bill recognizes a vocabulary word on a billboard when traveling.

Generalization is the occurrence of a learned behavior in the presence of a stimulus other than the one that produced the initial response. It is the expansion of a student's performance beyond the initial setting. Students must be able to expand or transfer what is learned to other settings (e.g., reading to math word problems, resource room to regular classroom). Generalization may be enhanced by the following:
- Use many examples in teaching to deepen application of learned skills.
- Use consistency in initial teaching situations and later introduce variety in format, procedure, and use of examples.
- Have the same information presented by different teachers, in different settings, and under varying conditions.
- Include a continuous reinforcement schedule at first, later changing to delayed and intermittent schedules as instruction progresses.
- Teach students to record instances of generalization and to reward themselves at that time.
- Associate naturally occurring stimuli when possible.

79. The effective teacher varies her instructional presentations and response requirements depending upon:
    (Easy) (Skill 3.3)

    A. Student needs
    B. The task at hand
    C. The learning situation
    D. All of the above

Answer: D. All of the above

An effective teacher examines student needs, the task at hand, and the learning situation when developing instructional presentations and response requirements.

80. For which stage of learning would computer software be utilized that allows for continued drill and practice of a skill to achieve accuracy and speed?
    (Average Rigor) (Skill 3.3)

    A. Acquisition
    B. Proficiency
    C. Maintenance
    D. Generalization

Answer: B. Proficiency

The four stages of learning are as follows:
- *Acquisition:* Introduction of a new skill
- *Maintenance:* Continued practice without further instruction
- *Proficiency:* Practice under supervision to achieve accuracy and speed
- *Generalization:* Application of the new skills in new settings and situations

81. Alan has failed repeatedly in his academic work. He needs continuous feedback in order to experience small, incremental achievements. What type of instructional material would best meet this need?
(Rigorous) (Skill 3.4)

   A. Programmed materials
   B. Audiotapes
   C. Materials with no writing required
   D. Worksheets

Answer: A. Programmed materials

Programmed materials are best suited, as Alan would be able to chart his progress as he achieves each goal. He can monitor himself and take responsibility for his successes.

82. After purchasing what seemed to be a very attractive new math kit for use with her SLD (specific learning disabled) students, Ms. Davis discovered her students could not use the kit unless she read the math problems and instructions to them, as the readability level was higher than the majority of the students' functional reading capabilities. Which criterion of the materials selection did Ms. Davis most likely fail to consider when selecting this math kit?
(Average Rigor) (Skill 3.4)

   A. Durability
   B. Relevance
   C. Component parts
   D. Price

Answer: B. Relevance

Relevance is the only cognitive factor listed. Since her students were severely learning disabled, she almost certainly would have considered the kit's durability and component parts. She did not have to consider price, as that would be taken care of by the district. To be fully relevant to a population, the material must be *accessible* to the population, and the reading level of the material made it inaccessible to her students.

83. Which of the following questions most directly evaluates the utility of instructional material?
(Rigorous) (Skill 3.4)

   A. Is the cost within budgetary means?
   B. Can the materials withstand handling by students?
   C. Are the materials organized in a useful manner?
   D. Are the needs of the students met by the use of the materials?

Answer: C. Are the materials organized in a useful manner?

It is a question of utility or usefulness.

84. A money bingo game was designed by Ms. Johnson for use with her middle grade students. Cards were constructed with different combinations of coins pasted on each of the nine spaces. Ms. Johnson called out various amounts of change (e.g., 30 cents), and students were instructed to cover the coin combinations on their cards, which equaled the amount of change (e.g., two dimes and two nickels, three dimes, and so on). The student who had the first bingo was required to add the coins in each of the spaces covered and tell the amounts before being declared the winner. Five of Ms. Johnson's sixth graders played the game during the ten-minute free activity time following math the first day the game was constructed. Which of the following attributes are present in this game in this situation?
(Average Rigor) (Skill 3.4)

   A. Accompanied by simple, uncomplicated rules
   B. Of brief duration, permitting replay
   C. Age appropriateness
   D. All of the above

Answer: D. All of the above

Games and puzzles should also be colorful and appealing, of relevance to individual students, and appropriate for learners at different skill levels in order to sustain interest and motivational value.

85. According to the three tier RTI model described by the Florida Center for Reading Research's (FCRR), students who need a moderate amount of help in one of the five critical areas of reading instruction in a general education class would receive additional reading instruction through the:
(Average Rigor) (Skill 5.7)

   A. Core reading program
   B. Intensive Intervention program
   C. Modified Reading program
   D. Supplemental reading program

Answer: D. Supplemental Reading Program.

Supplemental intervention programs provide help in one of the five critical areas of reading instruction: phonemic awareness, phonics, fluency, vocabulary, or comprehension. Children who have moderate needs will be in a second "tier" of assistance and will receive additional reading instruction each day. The intent is that these programs can be used to differentiate reading instruction in a general education setting, either through small group or individual work with the teacher or through additional staff assistance. The core reading program is the main program through which most children successfully achieve reading goals. Children who are two or more years behind grade level and who need much smaller group instruction or individual instruction on a much more intensive level, are in "tier 3," the *Intensive Intervention Program.*

86. Modifications of course material may take the form of:
(Average Rigor) (Skill 3.5)

   A. Simplifying texts
   B. Parallel curriculum
   C. Taped textbooks
   D. All of the above

Answer: D. All of the above

Materials, usually textbooks, are frequently modified because of reading level. The goal of modification is to present the material in a manner that the student can more readily understand, while preserving the basic ideas and content.

87. At which level of mathematics instruction will a child need to spend the most instructional and exploratory time in order to successfully master objectives?
(Average Rigor) (Skill 3.11)

   A. Symbolic Level
   B. Concept Level
   C. Mastery Level
   D. Connecting Level

Answer: B. Concept Level.

In order to internalize the concept, the child needs repeated and varied interaction with manipulatives at the concept level. it is important that, wherever possible, the child be led to *discover* the concept rather than having it stated by the teacher, then trying to memorize it. Following this stage, the child can begin to apply labels and representations *along with the manipulatives.* This stage forms a bridge, or *connecting level* to the last stage, the *symbolic level* when the child has internalized the concepts behind the symbols and can manipulate them to learn more without the support of more concrete scaffolding.

88. Which is a less than ideal example of collaboration in successful inclusion?
(Rigorous) (Skill 3.6)

   A. Special education teachers are part of the instructional team in a regular classroom.
   B. Special education teachers assist regular education teachers in the classroom.
   C. Teaming approaches are used for problem solving and program implementation.
   D. Regular teachers, special education teachers, and other specialists or support teachers co-teach.

Answer: B. Special education teachers assist regular education teachers in the classroom.

In a special education setting, the special education teacher should be the lead teacher.

89. **Janice requires occupational therapy and speech therapy services. She is your student. What must you do to insure her services are met?**
    (Rigorous) (Skill 3.6)

    A. Watch the services being rendered.
    B. Schedule collaboratively.
    C. Ask for services to be given in a push-in model.
    D. Ask them to train you to give the service.

Answer: B. Schedule collaboratively.

Collaborative scheduling of students to receive services is both your responsibility and that of the service provider. Scheduling together allows for both your convenience and that of the service provider. It also will provide you with an opportunity to make sure the student does not miss important information.

90. **What can you do to create a good working environment with a classroom assistant?**
    (Rigorous) (Skill 3.6)

    A. Plan lessons with the assistant.
    B. Write a contract that clearly defines his/her responsibilities in the classroom.
    C. Remove previously given responsibilities.
    D. All of the above

Answer: A. Plan lessons with the assistant.

Planning with your classroom assistant shows that you respect his/her input and allows you to see where he/she feels confident.

91. A paraprofessional has been assigned to assist you in the classroom. What action on the part of the teacher would lead to a poor working relationship?
(Average Rigor) (Skill 3.6)

    A. Having the paraprofessional lead a small group
    B. Telling the paraprofessional what you expect him/her to do
    C. Defining classroom behavior management as your responsibility alone
    D. Taking an active role in his/her evaluation

Answer: C. Defining classroom behavior management as your responsibility alone

When you do not allow another adult in the room to enforce the class rules, you create an environment where the other adult is seen as someone not to be respected. No one wants to be in a work environment where they do not feel respected.

92. Mrs. Freud is a consultant teacher. She has two students with Mr. Ricardo. Mrs. Freud should:
(Average Rigor) (Skill 3.6)

    A. Co-teach
    B. Spend two days a week in the classroom helping out.
    C. Discuss lessons with the teacher and suggest modifications before class.
    D. Pull her students out for instructional modifications.

Answer: C. Discuss lessons with the teacher and suggest modifications before class.

Consultant teaching provides the fewest interventions possible for the academic success of the academic child. Pushing in or pulling out are not essential components. However, an occasional observation as a classroom observer who does not single out any students may also be helpful in providing modifications for the student.

93. **In which way is a computer like an effective teacher?**
    (Average Rigor) (Skill 3.7)

    A. Provides immediate feedback
    B. Sets the pace at the rate of the average student
    C. Produces records of errors made only
    D. Programs to skill levels at which students at respective chronological ages should be working

Answer: A. Provides immediate feedback

The computer is a good tool for providing immediate feedback to the student. Immediate feedback increases motivation and lessens the risk that the student will practice the wrong answers.

94. **A Behavioral Intervention Plan (BIP):**
    (Rigorous) (Skill 4.4)

    A. Should be written by a team.
    B. Should be reviewed annually.
    C. Should be written by the teacher who is primarily responsible for the student.
    D. Should consider placement.

Answer: A. Should be written by a team.

IDEA 2004 establishes that the BIP is a team intervention. Writing BIPs without a team approach does not allow the behavior to truly be addressed as a team.

95. **Bill talks out in class an average of 15 times an hour. Other youngsters sometimes talk out, but Bill does so as a higher:**
    (Easy) (Skill 4.2)

    A. Rate
    B. Intensity
    C. Volume
    D. Degree

Answer: A. Rate

Rate or frequency is the number of times the behavior is displayed in a given period.

96. Which category of behaviors would most likely be found on a behavior rating scale?
(Easy) (Skill 4.3)

A. Disruptive, acting out
B. Shy, withdrawn
C. Aggressive (physical or verbal)
D. All of the above

Answer: D. All of the above

These are all possible problem behaviors that can adversely impact the student or the class; thus, they may be found on behavior rating scales.

97. In establishing your behavior management plan with the students, it is best to:
(Average Rigor) (Skill 4.3)

A. Have rules written and in place on day one.
B. Hand out a copy of the rules to the students on day one.
C. Have separate rules for each class on day one.
D. Have students involved in creating the rules on day one.

Answer: D. Have students involved in creating the rules on day one.

Rules are easier to follow when you not only know the reason they are in place, but you also took part in creating them. It may be good to already have a few rules pre-written and then to discuss if they cover all the rules the students have created. If not, it is possible you may want to modify your set of pre-written rules.

98. Bob shows behavior problems like lack of attention, being out of his seat, and talking out. His teacher has kept data on these behaviors and has found that Bob is showing much better self-control since he has been self-managing himself through a behavior modification program. The most appropriate placement recommendation for Bob at this time is probably:
(Easy) (Skill 4.4)

   A. Any available part-time special education program
   B. The regular classroom solely
   C. A behavior disorders resource room for one period a day
   D. A specific learning disabilities resource room for one period a day

Answer: B. The regular classroom solely

Bob is able to self-manage himself and is very likely to behave like the other children in the regular classroom. The classroom is the least restrictive environment.

99. A Behavior Intervention Plan (BIP) is based on the behaviorist assumption that many problem behaviors are:
(Average Rigor) (Skill 4.4)

   A. Predictable
   B. Observed
   C. Conditioned
   D. Learned

Answer: D. Learned

Behavior modification is based on the premise that most behavior, regardless of its appropriateness, has been learned, and therefore, can be changed.

100. Procedures employed to decrease targeted behaviors include:
(Rigorous) (Skill 4.4)

   A. Punishment
   B. Negative reinforcement
   C. Shaping
   D. Both A and B

Answer: A. Punishment

Punishment and extinction may be used to decrease target behaviors.

101. **Target behaviors must be:**
(Easy) (Skill 4.4)

   A. Observable
   B. Measurable
   C. Definable
   D. All of the above

Answer: D. All of the above

Behaviors must be observable, measurable, and definable in order to be assessed and changed.

102. **The most important step in writing a Functional Behavioral Assessment (FBA) is:**
(Rigorous) (Skill 4.4)

   A. Establish a replacement behavior.
   B. Establish levels of interventions.
   C. Establish antecedents related or causative to the behavior.
   D. Establish assessment periods of FBA effectiveness.

Answer: C. Establish antecedents related or causative to the behavior.

An FBA will only be successful if antecedents are recognized. Avoidance of situations and training/cultivating of replacement behaviors then become possible.

103. **Which description best characterizes primary reinforcers of an edible nature?**
(Average Rigor) (Skill 4.5)

   A. Natural
   B. Unconditioned
   C. Innately motivating
   D. All of the above

Answer: D. All of the above

Primary reinforcers are those stimuli that are of biological importance to an individual. They are natural, unlearned, unconditioned, and innately motivating. The most common and appropriate reinforcer used in the classroom is food.

104. **Mrs. Chang is trying to prevent satiation from occurring so that her reinforcers will be effective, as she is using a continuous reinforcement schedule. Which of the following ideas would be LEAST effective in preventing satiation?**
    (Rigorous) (Skill 4.5)

    A. Use only one type of edible rather than a variety.
    B. Ask for ten vocabulary words rather than twenty.
    C. Give pieces of cereal, bits of fruit, or M&Ms rather than large portions of edibles.
    D. Administer a peanut then a sip of water.

Answer: A. Use only one type of edible rather than a variety.

Here are some suggestions for preventing satiation:
- Vary reinforcers with instructional tasks.
- Shorten the instructional sessions, and presentation of reinforcers will be decreased.
- Alternate reinforcers (e.g., food, then juice).
- Decrease the size of edibles presented.
- Have an array of edibles available.

105. **Which tangible reinforcer would Mr. Whiting find to be MOST effective with teenagers?**
    (Easy) (Skill 4.5)

    A. Plastic whistle
    B. Winnie-the-Pooh book
    C. Poster of a current rock star
    D. Toy ring

Answer: C. Poster of a current rock star

This tops the list of things that teenagers crave. It is the most desirable.

106. **A positive reinforcer is generally effective if it is desired by the student and is:**
(Easy) (Skill 4.5)

   A. Worthwhile in size
   B. Given immediately after the desired behavior
   C. Given only upon the occurrence of the target behavior
   D. All of the above

Answer: D. All of the above

Timing and quality of the reinforcer are key to encouraging the individual to continue the targeted behavior.

107. **Dispensing school supplies is a component associated with which type of reinforcement system?**
(Average Rigor) (Skill 4.5)

   A. Activity reinforcement
   B. Tangible reinforcement
   C. Token reinforcement
   D. Both B and C

Answer: A. Activity reinforcement

The Premack Principle states that any activity in which a student voluntarily participates on a frequent basis can be used as a reinforcer for any activity in which the student seldom participates. Running errands, decorating bulletin boards, leading group activities, passing out books or papers, collecting materials, or operating equipment all provide activity reinforcement.

108. **Which type of reinforcement system is most easily generalized into other settings?**
    (Average Rigor) (Skill 4.5)

    A. Social reinforcement
    B. Activity reinforcement
    C. Tangible reinforcement
    D. Token reinforcement

Answer: A. Social reinforcement

There are many advantages to social reinforcement. It is easy to use, takes little of the teacher's time or effort, and is available in any setting. It is always positive, unlikely to satiate, and can be generalized to most situations.

109. **The Carrow Elicited Language Inventory is a test designed to give the examiner diagnostic information about a child's expressive grammatical competence. Which of the following language components is being assessed?**
    (Rigorous) (Skill 5.1)

    A. Phonology
    B. Morphology
    C. Syntax
    D. Both B and C

Answer: C. Syntax

- Morphology and syntax refer to understanding grammatical structure of language in the receptive channel and using the grammatical structure of language in the expressive channel.
- Assessment of morphology refers to linguistic structure of words.
- Assessment of syntax includes grammatical usage of word classes, word order, and transformational rules for the variance of word order in constructing sentences.

110. In the Grammatic Closure subtest of the Illinois Test of Psycholinguistic Abilities, the child is presented with a picture representing statements such as the following: "Here is one die; here are two ____." This test is essentially a test of:
(Rigorous) (Skill 5.1)

   A. Phonology
   B. Syntax
   C. Morphology
   D. Semantics

Answer: C. Morphology

Morphology refers to the rules governing the structure of words and how to put morphemes together to make words. "Dice" is the irregular plural form of "Die." Changing the ending to 'ce' is using a morphological structure. Syntax is a system of rules for sentence formation, not word formation.

111. Five-year-old Tom continues to substitute the "w" sound for the "r" sound when pronouncing words; therefore, he often distorts words, e.g., "wabbit" for "rabbit" and "wat" for "rat." His articulation disorder is basically a problem in:
(Average Rigor) (Skill 5.1)

   A. Phonology
   B. Morphology
   C. Syntax
   D. Semantics

Answer: A. Phonology

- Phonology: The study of significant units of speech sounds
- Morphology: The study of the smallest units of language that convey meaning
- Syntax: A system of rules for making grammatically-correct sentences
- Semantics: The study of the relationships between words and grammatical forms in a language and their underlying meaning

112. Which of the following is untrue about the ending "er" ?
    (Rigorous) (Skill 5.1)

    A. It is an example of a free morpheme.
    B. It represents one of the smallest units of meaning within a word.
    C. It is called an inflectional ending.
    D. When added to a word, it connotes a comparative status.

Answer: A. It is an example of a free morpheme.

A morpheme is the smallest unit of meaningful language. A free morpheme has meaning that can stand alone as a word. "Er," on its own, has no meaning. It is a bound morpheme, and is affixed to a free morpheme to alter its meaning.

113. Which component of language involves language content rather than the form of language?
    (Rigorous) (Skill 5.1)

    A. Phonology
    B. Morphology
    C. Semantics
    D. Syntax

Answer: C. Semantics

Semantics is the study of the relationships between words and grammatical forms in a language and their underlying meaning.

114. The social skills of students in mental retardation programs are likely to be appropriate for children of their mental age, rather than chronological age. This means that the teacher will need to do all of the following EXCEPT:
    (Easy) (Skill 5.2)

    A. Model desired behavior.
    B. Provide clear instructions.
    C. Expect age-appropriate behaviors.
    D. Adjust the physical environment when necessary.

Answer: C. Expect age-appropriate behaviors

Age appropriate means mental age appropriate, not chronological age appropriate.

115. Which of the following is a language disorder?
(Average Rigor) (Skill 5.2)

   A. Articulation problems
   B. Stuttering
   C. Aphasia
   D. Excessive Nasality

Answer: C. Aphasia

Language disorders are often considered just one category of speech disorder. The problem is really different, with its own origins and causes. Persons with language disorders exhibit one or more of the following traits:
- Difficulty in comprehending questions, commands, or statements (receptive language problems)
- Inability to adequately express their own thoughts (expressive language problems)
- Language that is below the level expected for the child's chronological age (delayed language)
- Interrupted language development (dysphasia)
- Qualitatively different language
- Total absence of language

116. Which of the following is a speech disorder?
(Average Rigor) (Skill 5.2)

   A. Disfluency
   B. Aphasia
   C. Delayed language
   D. Comprehension difficulties

Answer: A. Disfluency

Persons with speech disorders exhibit one or more of the following traits:
- Unintelligible speech or speech that is difficult to understand, and articulation disorders (distortions, omissions, substitutions)
- Speech-flow disorders (sequence, duration, rate, rhythm, fluency)
- Unusual voice quality (nasality, breathiness, hoarseness, pitch, intensity, quality disorders)
- Obvious emotional discomfort when trying to communicate (stuttering, cluttering)
- Damage to nerves or brain centers which control muscles used in speech (dysarthria).

117. Which of the following is an example of cross-modal perception involving integrating visual stimuli to an auditory verbal process?
(Rigorous) (Skill 5.3)

   A. Following spoken directions
   B. Describing a picture
   C. Finding certain objects in pictures
   D. Both B and C

Answer: B. Describing a picture

We see (visual modality) the picture and use words (auditory modality) to describe it.

118. Matthew's conversational speech is adequate, but when he tries to speak before a group of more than two listeners, his speech becomes mumbling and halting. Which of the following activities would be LEAST helpful in strengthening Matthew's self-expression skills?
(Rigorous) (Skill 5.3)

   A. Having him participate in show-and-tell time
   B. Asking him comprehension questions about a story that was read to the class
   C. Having him recite a poem in front of the class, with two other children
   D. Asking him to tell a joke to the rest of the class

Answer: B. Asking him comprehension questions about a story that was read to class.

Answering the teacher's questions emphasizes speaking in front of one other person (the teacher) and does not expand his comfort zone to a larger group. The other activities require him to speak in front of more people.

119. **All of the modes listed below are primary categories of Augmentative Alternative Communication EXCEPT:**
(Easy) (Skill 5.4)

   A. Wheelchairs
   B. Graphical communication boards
   C. Eye gaze techniques
   D. Sign language

Answer: A. Wheelchairs

The primary purpose of a wheelchair is mobility, not communication.

120. **A functional curriculum includes:**
(Average Rigor) (Skill 6.1)

   A. Regents curriculum
   B. Life skills
   C. Remedial academics
   D. Vocational placement

Answer: B. Life skills

While a, c and, d may be utilized in the functional curriculum, the curriculum may not be considered functional without addressing life skills.

121. **Donna has been labeled "learning disabled" since second grade and has developed a fear of not being able to keep up with her peers. She has just entered middle school with a poor self-concept and often acts out to cover up her fear of failure. What is the most appropriate action her teacher can take when Donna exhibits minor inappropriate behavior?**
(Rigorous) (Skill 6.1)

   A. Ignore the behavior unless it is too dangerous or distracting.
   B. Praise her for her correct behavior and responses.
   C. Discuss the inappropriate behavior tactfully and in private.
   D. All of the above.

Answer: D. All of the above

All three of the actions listed will help correct the minor inappropriate behavior, while at the same time helping to improve the child's self-concept.

122. **Which of the following is the first step you should take to prepare to teach preparation for social situations?**
(Average Rigor) (Skill 6.1)

   A. Allow students to plan events.
   B. Lecture.
   C. Anticipate possible problems.
   D. Take your students to the anticipated setting.

Answer: C. Anticipate possible problems.

Look at all the things that could go wrong first. Chances are that if you are not prepared, an embarrassing situation could occur.

123. **Children with disabilities are LEAST likely to improve their social-interpersonal skills by:**
(Rigorous) (Skill 6.1)

   A. Developing sensitivity to other people
   B. Making behavioral choices in social situations
   C. Developing social maturity
   D. Talking with their sister or brother

Answer: D. Talking with their sister or brother

The social skills of the child are known in the family and seen as "normal" for him/her. Regular conversation with a family member would be the least conducive to improving social skills. Remember, the purpose in building social-interpersonal skills is to improve a person's ability to maintain interdependent relationships between persons.

124. When you need to evaluate a student's work ethics, you should give what assessment?
(Rigorous) (Skill 6.2)

    A. Naturalistic
    B. Dynamic
    C. Performance-based
    D. Criterion-referenced

Answer: A. Naturalistic

Work ethics are social skills. Social skills are best evaluated over time in their natural surroundings.

125. One of the most important goals of the special education teacher is to foster and create with the student:
(Easy) (Skill 6.3)

    A. Handwriting skills
    B. Self-advocacy
    C. An increased level of reading
    D. Logical reasoning

Answer: B. Self-advocacy

When a student achieves the ability to recognize his/her deficits and knows how to correctly advocate for his/her needs, the child has learned one of the most important life skills.

126. **In career education, specific training and preparation required for the world of work occurs during the phase of:**
    (Average Rigor) (Skill 7.1)

    A. Career awareness
    B. Career exploration
    C. Career preparation
    D. Daily living and personal-social interaction

Answer: C. Career preparation

Curricular aspects of career education include:
- *career awareness:* diversity of available jobs
- *career exploration:* skills needed for occupational groups
- *career preparation:* specific training and preparation required for the world of work

127. **The transition activities that have to be addressed, unless the IEP team finds them uncalled for, are:**
    (Average Rigor) (Skill 7.2)

    A. Instruction
    B. Community experiences
    C. The development of objectives related to employment and other post-school areas
    D. All of the above

Answer: D. All of the above

Transition services will be different for each student, but all three aspects must be addressed. Transition services must take into account the student's interests and preferences. Evaluation of career interests, aptitudes, skills, and training may be considered.

128. **The most important member of the transition team is the:**
(Easy) (Skill 7.3)

   A. Parent
   B. Student
   C. Secondary personnel
   D. Postsecondary personnel

Answer: B. Student

Transition planning is a student-centered event that necessitates a collaborative endeavor. Responsibilities are shared by the student, parents, secondary personnel, and postsecondary personnel, who are all members of the transition team; however, it is important that the student play a key role in transition planning. This will entail asking the student to identify preferences and interests and to attend meetings on transition planning. The degree of success experienced by the student in postsecondary educational settings depends on the student's degree of motivation, independence, self-direction, self-advocacy, and academic abilities developed in high school. Student participation in transition activities should be implemented as early as possible and no later than age 16.

129. **Vocational training programs are based on all of the following ideas EXCEPT:**
(Average Rigor) (Skill 7.4)

   A. Students obtain career training from elementary through high school.
   B. Students acquire specific training in job skills prior to exiting school.
   C. Students need specific training and supervision in applying skills learned in school to requirements in job situations.
   D. Students obtain needed instruction and field-based experiences that help them to be able to work in specific occupations.

Answer: A. Students obtain career training from elementary through high school.

Vocational education programs or transition programs prepare students for entry into the labor force. They are usually incorporated into the work-study at the high school or post-secondary levels. They are usually focused on job skills, job opportunities, skill requirements for specific jobs, personal qualifications in relation to job requirements, work habits, money management, and academic skills needed for specific jobs.

130. **What is MOST descriptive of vocational training in special education?** *(Easy) (Skill 7.4)*

   A. Trains students in intellectual disabilities solely.
   B. Segregates students with and without disabilities in vocational training programs.
   C. Only includes students capable of moderate supervision.
   D. Instruction focuses upon self-help skills, social-interpersonal skills, motor skills, rudimentary academic skills, simple occupational skills, and lifetime leisure and occupational skills

Answer: D. Instruction focuses upon self-help skills, social-interpersonal skills, motor skills, rudimentary academic skills, simple occupational skills, and lifetime leisure and occupational skills.

Persons with disabilities are mainstreamed with non-disabled students where possible. Special sites provide training for those persons with more severe disabilities who are unable to be successfully taught in an integrated setting. Specially-trained vocational counselors monitor and supervise student work sites.

Post-test

DIRECTIONS: Read each item and select the best response.

1. The minimum number of IEP meetings required per year is:
   (Average Rigor) (Skill 1.1)

   A. As many as necessary
   B. One
   C. Two
   D. Three

2. Which of these groups is not comprehensively covered by IDEA?
   (Average Rigor) (Skill 1.1)

   A. Gifted and talented
   B. Mentally retarded
   C. Specific learning disabled
   D. Speech and language impaired

3. Educators who advocate educating all children in their neighborhood classrooms and schools, who propose the end of labeling and segregation of special needs students in special classes, and who call for the delivery of special supports and services directly in the classroom may be said to support the:
   (Rigorous) (Skill 1.7)

   A. Full service model
   B. Regular education initiative
   C. Full inclusion model
   D. Mainstream model

4. Section 504 differs from the scope of IDEA because its main focus is on:
   (Rigorous) (Skill 1.1)

   A. Prohibition of discrimination on the basis of disability
   B. A basis for additional support services and accommodations in a special education setting
   C. Procedural rights and safeguards for the individual
   D. Federal funding for educational services

5. **Public Law 99-457 amended the EHA to make provisions for:**
(Easy) (Skill 1.1)

   A. Education services for "uneducable" children
   B. Educational services for children in jail settings
   C. Special Education benefits for children birth to five years old
   D. Education services for medically fragile children

6. **Under the provisions of IDEA, the student is entitled to all of these EXCEPT:**
(Easy) (Skill 1.1)

   A. Placement in the best environment
   B. Placement in the least restrictive environment
   C. Provision of educational needs at no cost
   D. Provision of individualized, appropriate educational program

7. **Students who recognize and name some letters, apply sounds to many of the consonants, and do some invented spelling, but do not recognize common spelling patterns are in which phase of learning to decode?**
(Average rigor) (Skill 5.10)

   A. Pre-alphabetic phase
   B. Partial alphabetic phase
   C. Full- alphabetic phase
   D. Consolidated alphabetic phase

8. **The following words all describe an IEP objective EXCEPT:**
(Easy) (Skill 1.1)

   A. Specific
   B. Observable
   C. Measurable
   D. Criterion-referenced

9. **Which of the following statements was not offered as a rationale for the Regular Education Intervention (REI) or inclusion?** *(Rigorous) (Skill 1.1)*

   A. Special education students are not usually identified until their learning problems have become severe.
   B. Lack of funding will mean that support for the special needs children will not be available in the regular classroom.
   C. Putting children in segregated special education placements is stigmatizing.
   D. There are students with learning or behavior problems who do not meet special education requirements but who still need special services.

10. Hector is a 10th grader in a program for the severely emotionally handicapped. After a classmate taunted him about his mother, Hector threw a desk at the other boy and attacked him. As a crisis intervention team attempted to break up the fight, one teacher hurt his knee. The other boy received a concussion. Hector now faces disciplinary measures. How long can he be suspended without the suspension constituting a "change of placement"?
(Average Rigor) (Skill 1.1)

A. 5 days
B. 10 days
C. 10 + 30 days
D. 60 days

11. The concept that a handicapped student cannot be expelled for misconduct that is a manifestation of the handicap itself is not limited to students who are labeled "seriously emotionally disturbed." Which reason does NOT explain this concept?
(Easy) (Skill 1.1)

A. Emphasis on individualized evaluation.
B. Consideration of the problems and needs of handicapped students.
C. Right to a free and appropriate public education.
D. Putting these students out of school will just leave them on the streets to commit crimes.

12. Jonathan has Attention Deficit Hyperactivity Disorder (ADHD). He is in a regular classroom and appears to be doing okay. However, his teacher does not want John in her class because he will not obey her when she asks him to stop doing a repetitive action such as tapping his foot. The teacher sees this as distracting during tests. John needs:
(Easy) (Skill 1.1)

A. An IEP
B. A 504 Plan
C. A VESID evaluation
D. A more restrictive environment

13. **IDEA 2004 stated that there is a disproportionate number of minority students classified as needing special education services. IDEA 2004 suggests this is due to:**
(Average Rigor) (Skill 1.1)

    A. Socioeconomic status where disproportionate numbers exist
    B. Improper evaluations – not making allowances for students who have English as a second language
    C. Growing population of minorities
    D. Percentage of drug abuse per ethnicity

14. **NCLB and IDEA 2004 changed special Education teacher requirements by:**
(Easy) (Skill 1.1)

    A. Requiring a highly-qualified status for job placement
    B. Adding changes to the requirement for certifications
    C. Adding legislation requiring teachers to maintain knowledge of law
    D. Requiring inclusive environmental experience prior to certification

15. **Which law specifically states that, "Full Inclusion is not the only way for a student to reach his/her highest potential"?**
(Rigorous) (Skill 1.1)

    A. IDEA
    B. IDEA 97
    C. IDEA 2004
    D. Part 200

16. **NCLB (No Child Left Behind Act) was signed on January 8, 2002. It addresses what?**
(Rigorous) (Skill 1.1)

    A. Accessibility of curriculum to the student
    B. Administrative incentives for school improvements
    C. The funding to provide services required
    D. Accountability of school personnel for student achievement

17. **IDEA 97 changed IDEA by requiring:**
(Rigorous) (Skill 1.1)

    A. IEPs to be in electronic format
    B. Requiring all staff working with the student to have access to the IEP
    C. Allowing past assessments to be used in Triennials
    D. BIPs for many students with FBAs

18. **What legislation started FAPE?**
(Rigorous) (Skill 1.1)

   A. Section 504
   B. EHCA
   C. IDEA
   D. Education Amendment 1974

19. **According to the National Reading Panel, which of the following activities would NOT be a best practice for increasing phoneme awareness?**
(Average) (Skill 5.11)

   A. Oral rhyming games
   B. Matching oral words based on the beginning, middle, or ending sound.
   C. Singing songs like "Knick, Knack, Paddy Whack" where single sounds are rearranged or changed
   D. Using letter tiles to spell out simple words

20. **The revision of Individuals with Disabilities Education Act in 1997 required:**
(Rigorous) (Skill 1.1)

   A. Collaboration of educational professionals in order to provide equitable opportunities for students with disabilities.
   B. Removed the requirement for short-term objectives for objectives with goals.
   C. School administrator approval for an IEP to be put into place.
   D. FBAs and BIPs for all students who were suspended for 6 days.

21. **A person who has a learning disability has:**
(Easy) (Skill 1.1)

   A. An IQ two standard deviations below the norm
   B. Congenital abnormalities
   C. Is limited by the educational environment
   D. Has a disorder in one of the basic psychological processes

22. **IDEA 2004 changed the IEP by?**
(Rigorous) (Skill 1.1)

   A. Not requiring short-term objectives
   B. Requiring an inclusive activity
   C. Requiring parents to participate in the CSE
   D. Establishing new criteria to be classified as learning disabled

23. **According to IDEA 2004, students with disabilities are to do what?**
    (Average Rigor) (Skill 1.1)

    A. Participate in the general education program to the fullest extent that it is beneficial for them
    B. Participate in a vocational training within the general education setting
    C. Participate in a general education setting for physical education
    D. Participate in a modified program that meets his/her needs

24. **Satisfaction of the LRE requirement means that:**
    (Easy) (Skill 1.2)

    A. The school is providing the best services it can offer there.
    B. The school is providing the best services the district has to offer.
    C. The student is being educated with the fewest special education services necessary..
    D. The student is being educated in the least restrictive setting that meets his or her needs

25. **A review of a student's eligibility for an exceptional student program must be done:**
    (Average Rigor) (Skill 1.2)

    A. At least once every 3 years
    B. At least once a year
    C. Only if a major change occurs in academic or behavioral performance
    D. When a student transfers to a new school

26. **Which of the following would be effective techniques for improving fluency?**
    (Easy Rigor) (Skill 5.13)

    A. Choral reading
    B. Reader's theatre
    C. Modeling and recorded books
    D. All of the above

27. **Lack of regular follow-up, difficulty in transporting materials, and lack of consistent support for students who need more assistance are disadvantages of which type of service model?**
    (Rigorous) (Skill 1.2)

    A. Regular classroom
    B. Consultant with regular teacher
    C. Itinerant
    D. Resource room

28. **Ability to supply individualized instructional materials, programs, and methods and to influence environmental learning variables on a regular basis in a mainstream classroom are advantages of which service model for exceptional students?** *(Average Rigor) (Skill 1.2)*

    A. Regular classroom
    B. Consultant teacher
    C. Itinerant teacher
    D. Resource room

29. **An emphasis on instructional remediation and individualized instruction in problem areas and a focus on mainstreaming students in areas that are not a problem are characteristics of which model of service delivery?** *(Average Rigor) (Skill 1.2)*

    A. Regular classroom
    B. Consultant teacher
    C. Itinerant teacher
    D. Resource room

30. **Which of these would not be considered a valid attempt to contact a parent for an IEP meeting?** *(Average Rigor) (Skill 1.2)*

    A. Telephone call
    B. Copy of correspondence
    C. Message left on an answering machine
    D. Record of home visits

31. **Cheryl is a 15-year-old student receiving educational services in a full-time EH classroom. The date for her IEP review will take place two months before her 16th birthday. According to the requirements of IDEA, what must ADDITIONALLY be included in this review?** *(Average Rigor) (Skill 1.2)*

    A. Graduation plan
    B. Individualized transition plan
    C. Individualized family service plan
    D. Transportation planning

32. **Most students with disabilities develop better self-images and recognize their own academic and social strengths when they are:** *(Easy) (Skill 1.2)*

    A. Included in the mainstream classroom
    B. Provided community-based internships
    C. Socializing in the hallway
    D. Provided 1:1 instructional opportunity

33. **A best practice for evaluating student performance and progress on IEPs is:**
    (Average Rigor) (Skill 2.3)

    A. Standardized assessment
    B. Criterion-based assessment
    C. Rating scales
    D. Norm-referenced assessment

34. **Guidelines for an Individualized Family Service Plan (IFSP) would be described in which legislation?**
    (Rigorous) (Skill 1.3)

    A. PL 94-142 (Education for the Handicapped Act)
    B. PL 99-457 (IDEA 2000)
    C. PL 101-476 IDEA 1990)
    D. ADA

35. **Which of these characteristics is NOT included in the P.L. 94-142 definition of emotional disturbance:**
    (Rigorous) (Skill 1.4)

    A. General pervasive mood of unhappiness or depression
    B. Social maladjustment manifested in a number of settings
    C. Tendency to develop physical symptoms, pains, or fear associated with school or personal problems
    D. Inability to learn that is not attributed to intellectual, sensory, or health factors

36. Justin is diagnosed with autism and is in an inclusive setting. You were called down to "Stop him from turning the lights off and remove him." When you arrive, you learn that today a movie was supposed to be finished, but the VCR broke, so the teacher planned another activity. What is the best way to explain to the teacher why Justin was turning off the lights?
(Easy) (Skill 1.4)

    A. He is perseverating and will stop shortly.
    B. He is telling you the lights bother him.
    C. He needs forewarning before a transition. Next time you have an unexpected change in classroom schedule, please let him know.
    D. Please understand that this is part of who Justin is. He will leave the lights alone after I talk to him.

37. According to IDEA, a child whose disability is related to being deaf and blind may not be classified as:
(Rigorous) (Skill 1.4)

    A. Multiply Disabled
    B. Other Health Impaired
    C. Mentally Retarded
    D. Visually Impaired

38. A child may be classified under the special education "umbrella" as having Traumatic Brain Injury (TBI) if he/she does not have the following cause?
(Rigorous) (Skill 1.4)

    A. Stroke
    B. Anoxia
    C. Encephalitis
    D. Birth trauma

39. In mainstream America, which body language would not likely be interpreted as a sign of defensiveness, aggression, or hostility?
(Rigorous) (Skill 1.5)

    A. Pointing
    B. Direct eye contact
    C. Hands on hips
    D. Arms crossed

40. Of the various factors that contribute to delinquency and antisocial behavior, which has been found to be the weakest?
(Rigorous) (Skill 1.5)

    A. Criminal behavior and/or alcoholism in the father
    B. Lax mother and punishing father
    C. Socioeconomic disadvantage
    D. Long history of broken home or marital discord among parents

41. Poor moral development, lack of empathy, and behavioral excesses, such as aggression, are the most obvious characteristics of which behavioral disorder?
    (Average Rigor) (Skill 1.5)

    A. Autism
    B. ADD-H
    C. Conduct disorder
    D. Pervasive development disorder

42. School refusal, obsessive-compulsive disorders, psychosis, and separation anxiety are also frequently accompanied by:
    (Rigorous) (Skill 1.5)

    A. Conduct disorder
    B. ADHD
    C. Depression
    D. Autism

43. Signs of depression do not typically include:
    (Easy) (Skill 1.5)

    A. Hyperactivity
    B. Changes in sleep patterns
    C. Recurring thoughts of death or suicide
    D. Significant changes in weight or appetite

44. Children who are characterized by impulsivity generally:
    (Easy) (Skill 1.5)

    A. Do not feel sorry for their actions
    B. Blame others for their actions
    C. Do not weigh alternatives before acting
    D. Do not outgrow their problem

45. Which of these is listed as only a minor scale on the Behavior Problem Checklist?
    (Average Rigor) (Skill 1.5)

    A. Motor excess
    B. Conduct disorder
    C. Socialized aggression
    D. Anxiety withdrawal

46. Which of these explanations would not likely account for the lack of a clear definition of behavior disorders?
    (Rigorous) (Skill 1.5)

    A. Problems with measurement
    B. Cultural and/or social influences and views of what is acceptable
    C. The numerous types of manifestations of behavior disorders
    D. Differing theories that use their own terminology and definitions

47. Ryan is 3, and her temper tantrums last for an hour. Bryan is 8, and he does not stay on task for more than 10 minutes without teacher prompts. These behaviors differ form normal children in terms of their:
(Average Rigor) (Skill 1.5)

    A. Rate
    B. Topography
    C. Duration
    D. Magnitude

48. All children cry, hit, fight, and play alone at different times. Children with behavior disorders will perform these behaviors at a higher than normal:
(Average Rigor) (Skill 1.5)

    A. Rate
    B. Topography
    C. Duration
    D. Magnitude

49. The exhibition of two or more types of problem behaviors across different areas of functioning is known as:
(Rigorous) (Skill 1.5)

    A. Multiple maladaptive behaviors
    B. Clustering
    C. Social maladjustment
    D. Conduct disorder

50. Children with behavior disorders often do not exhibit stimulus control. This means that they have not learned:
(Easy) (Skill 1.5)

    A. The right things to do
    B. Where and when certain behaviors are appropriate
    C. Right from wrong
    D. Listening skills

51. Truancy, gang membership, and feelings of pride in belonging to a delinquent subculture are indicative of:
(Rigorous) (Skill 1.5)

    A. Conduct disorder
    B. Personality disorders
    C. Immaturity
    D. Socialized aggression

52. Which of these is not true for most children with behavior disorders?
(Rigorous) (Skill 1.5)

    A. Many score in the "slow learner" or "mildly retarded" range on IQ tests.
    B. They are frequently behind their classmates in terms of academic achievement.
    C. They are bright but bored with their surroundings.
    D. A large amount of time is spent on nonproductive, nonacademic behaviors.

53. Echolalia, repetitive stereotyped actions, and a severe disorder of thinking and communication are indicative of:
(Average Rigor) (Skill 1.5)

    A. Psychosis
    B. Schizophrenia
    C. Autism
    D. Paranoia

54. Which behavioral disorder is difficult to diagnose in children because the symptoms are manifested quite differently than in adults?
(Rigorous) (Skill 1.5)

    A. Anorexia
    B. Schizophrenia
    C. Paranoia
    D. Depression

55. Tom's special education teacher became concerned about her ability to deliver the adaptations and services Tom needs when she heard him begin to talk to someone who was not there. Tom also responds to questions in a nonsensical manner. Tom's teacher is concerned because she thinks he may be exhibiting symptoms of:
(Easy) (Skill 1.5)

    A. Sensory perceptual disorder
    B. Mental illnesses
    C. Depression
    D. Tactile sensory deprivation

56. Janice is a new student in your self-contained class. She is extremely quiet and makes little if any eye contact. Yesterday, she started to "parrot" what another student said. Today, you became concerned when she did not follow directions and seemed not to even recognize your presence. Her cumulative file arrived today; when you review the health section, it most likely will state that she is diagnosed with:
(Average Rigor) (Skill 1.5)

    A. Autism
    B. Central Processing Disorder
    C. Traumatic Brain Injury
    D. Mental Retardation

57. The National Reading Panel (2000) Report identified all of these as critical areas of reading instruction EXCEPT:
(Average Rigor) (Skill 5.9)

    A. Phoneme Awareness
    B. Fluency
    C. Memory
    D. Vocabulary

58. Which one of the following is NOT a primary purpose of an IEP?
(Rigorous) (Skill 1.6)

    A. To outline instructional programs
    B. To develop self-advocacy skills
    C. To function as the basis for evaluation
    D. To facilitate communication among staff members, teachers, parents, and students

59. Kara's mother has requested a computer for her child to do class work and homework, but the IEP Team does not agree. Kara complains to you. You should:
(Easy) (Skill 1.6)

    A. Tell her you agree with her.
    B. Recommend an outside source that may provide a free laptop computer.
    C. Tell Kara's mother she can still fight the team's decision by requesting a due process hearing.
    D. Tell the parent to call a lawyer.

60. Shyquan is in your inclusive class, and she exhibits a slower comprehension of assigned tasks and concepts. Her first two grades were Bs, but she is now receiving failing marks. She has seen the resource teacher. You should:
(Rigorous) (Skill 1.7)

    A. Ask for a review of current placement
    B. Tell Shyquan to seek extra help
    C. Ask Shyquan if she is frustrated
    D. Ask the regular education teacher to slow instruction

61. In exceptional student education, assessment is used to make decisions about all of the following EXCEPT:
(Average Rigor) (Skill 2.1)

    A. Screening and initial identification of children who may need services
    B. Selection and evaluation of teaching strategies and programs
    C. Determining the desired attendance rate of a student
    D. Development of goals, objectives, and evaluation for the IEP

62. The extent to which a test measures what it claims to measure is called:
    (Easy) (Skill 2.3)

    A. Reliability
    B. Validity
    C. Factor analysis
    D. Chi square

63. The purpose of error analysis of a test is to:
    (Easy) (Skill 2.3)

    A. Determine what events were labeled in error.
    B. Determine if the test length was the cause of error.
    C. Evaluate the types of errors made by categorizing incorrect answers.
    D. Establish a baseline

64. Which would not be an advantage of using a criterion-referenced test?
    (Average Rigor) (Skill 2.3)

    A. You can use the results to evaluate the effectiveness of your teaching methods.
    B. It can pinpoint exact areas of weaknesses and strengths.
    C. You can design them yourself.
    D. You can compare your students to the national norm.

65. Which is NOT an example of a standard score?
    (Average Rigor) (Skill 2.4)

    A. T Score
    B. Z Score
    C. Standard deviation
    D. Stanine

66. The most direct method of obtaining assessment data, and perhaps the most objective, is:
    (Rigorous) (Skill 2.5)

    A. Testing
    B. Self-recording
    C. Observation
    D. Experimenting

67. The National Reading Panel Report (2000) reviewed research showing that direct instruction in vocabulary is essential, and that:
    (Average Rigor) (Skill 5.15)

    A. Learning vocabulary in the specific context in which it is to be used is the most effective technique.
    B. Use of word maps is the most effective strategy for teaching vocabulary mastery.
    C. Using a variety of methods and approaches is far more effective than dependence upon a single approach to instruction.
    D. Noncontextual vocabulary strategies are the most effective methods for long term retention of vocabulary content.

68. Alternative assessments include all of the following EXCEPT:
(Average Rigor) (Skill 2.5)

    A. Portfolios
    B. Interviews
    C. Standardized tests
    D. Performance-based tests

69. Which of the following is NOT one of the three aspects of the issue of fair assessment for individuals from minority groups that Slavia and Ysseldyke, 1995, point out as particularly relevant to the assessment of students?
(Rigorous) (Skill 2.6)

    A. Representation
    B. Diversity
    C. Acculturation
    D. Language

70. The Premack principle of increasing the performance of a less-preferred activity by immediately following it with a highly-preferred activity is the basis of:
(Rigorous) (Skill 3.2)

    A. Response cost
    B. Token systems
    C Contingency contracting
    D. Self-recording management

71. A suggested amount of time for a large-group instruction lesson for a sixth- or seventh-grade group would be:
(Rigorous) (Skill 3.2)

    A. 5 to 40 minutes
    B. 5 to 50 minutes
    C. 5 to 30 minutes
    D. 5 to 15 minutes

72. In a positive classroom environment, errors are viewed as:
(Easy) (Skill 3.2)

    A. Symptoms of deficiencies
    B. Lack of attention or ability
    C. A natural part of the learning process
    D. The result of going too fast

73. Which of the following should be considered when planning the spatial arrangement of your classroom?
(Average Rigor) (Skill 3.2)

    A. Adequate physical space
    B. Lighting characteristics
    C. Window location
    D. All of the above

74. Cooperative learning does NOT utilize?
(Average Rigor) (Skill 3.2)

    A. Shared ideas
    B. Small groups
    C. Independent practice
    D. Student expertise

75. **Which type of grouping arrangement would be most effective for teaching basic academic skills such as math facts or reading?**
(Rigorous) (Skill 3.2)

   A. Large group with teacher
   B. Peer tutoring
   C. Small group instruction
   D. Cooperative learning

76. **If the arrangement in a fixed-ratio schedule of reinforcement is 3, when will the student receive the reinforcer?**
(Rigorous) (Skill 3.3)

   A. After every third correct response
   B. After every third correct response in a row
   C. After the third correct response in the time interval of the behavior sample
   D. After the third correct response even if the undesired behavior occurs in between correct responses

77. **Laura is beginning to raise her hand first instead of talking out. An effective schedule of reinforcement would be:**
(Rigorous) (Skill 3.3)

   A. Continuous
   B. Variable
   C. Intermittent
   D. Fixed

78. **As Laura continues to raise her hand to speak, the teacher would want to change to this schedule of reinforcement in order to wean her from reinforcement:**
(Rigorous) (Skill 3.3)

   A. Continuous
   B. Variable
   C. Intermittent
   D. Fixed

79. **Laura has demonstrated that she has mastered the goal of raising her hand to speak; reinforcement during the maintenance phase should be:**
(Rigorous) (Skill 3.3)

   A. Continuous
   B. Variable
   C. Intermittent
   D. Fixed

80. **A student may have great difficulty in meeting a target goal if the teacher has not first considered:**
(Rigorous) (Skill 3.3)

   A. If the student has external or internal locus of control
   B. If the student is motivated to attain the goal
   C. If the student has the essential prerequisite skills to perform the goal
   D. If the student has had previous success or failure meeting the goal in other classes

81. Justin, a second grader, is reinforced if he is on task at the end of each 10-minute block of time that the teacher observes him. This is an example of what type of reinforcement schedule?
(Average Rigor) (Skill 3.3)

    A. Continuous
    B. Fixed interval
    C. Fixed ratio
    D. Variable ratio

82. At the beginning of the school year, Annette had a problem with being late to class. Her teacher reinforced her each time she was in her seat when the bell rang. In October, her teacher decided to reward her every other day when she was not tardy to class. This reinforcement schedule would be:
(Rigorous) (Skill 3.3)

    A. Continuous
    B. Fixed interval
    C. Variable ratio
    D. Fixed ratio

83. By November, Annette's teacher is satisfied with her record of being on time and decides to change the schedule of reinforcement. The best type of reinforcement schedule for maintenance of behavior is:
(Average Rigor) (Skill 3.3)

    A Continuous
    B. Fixed interval
    C. Variable ratio
    D. Fixed Ratio

84. Transfer of learning occurs when?
(Rigorous) (Skill 3.3)

    A. Experience with one task influences performance on another task.
    B. Content can be explained orally.
    C. Student experiences the "I got it!" syndrome.
    D. Curricular objective is exceeded.

85. To facilitate learning instructional objectives:
(Average Rigor) (Skill 3.3)

    A. They should be taken from a grade-level spelling list.
    B. They should be written and shared.
    C. They should be arranged in order of similarity.
    D. They should be taken from a scope and sequence.

86. **Marisol has been mainstreamed into a ninth grade language arts class. Although her behavior is satisfactory and she likes the class, Marisol's reading level is about two years below grade level. The class has been assigned to read *Great Expectations* and to write a report. What intervention would be LEAST successful in helping Marisol complete this assignment?**
(Average Rigor) (Skill 3.5)

   A. Having Marisol listen to a taped recording while following the story in the regular text
   B. Giving her a modified version of the story
   C. Telling her to choose a different book that she can read
   D. Showing a film to the entire class and comparing and contrasting it to the book

87. **Teacher modeling, student-teacher dialogues, and peer interactions are part of which teaching technique designed to provide support during the initial phases of instruction?**
(Rigorous) (Skill 3.5)

   A. Reciprocal teaching
   B. Scaffolding
   C. Peer tutoring
   D. Cooperative learning

88. **Grading should be based on all of the following EXCEPT:**
(Average Rigor) (Skill 3.5)

   A. Clearly-defined mastery of course objectives
   B. A variety of evaluation methods
   C. Performance of the student in relation to other students
   D. Assigning points for activities and basing grades on a point total

89. **Which of the following sentences will NOT test recall?**
(Average Rigor) (Skill 3.5)

   A. What words in the story describe Goldilocks?
   B. Why did Goldilocks go into the three bears' house?
   C. Name in order the things that belonged to the three bears that Goldilocks tried.
   D. What did the three bears learn about leaving their house unlocked?

90. Which is not a goal of collaborative consultation?
(Average Rigor) (Skill 3.6)

   A. Prevent learning and behavior problems with mainstreamed students
   B. Coordinate the instructional programs between mainstream and Exceptional Student Education classes
   C. Facilitate solutions to learning and behavior problems
   D. Function as an ESE service model

91. An important goal of collaborative consultation is:
(Easy) (Skill 3.6)

   A. Mainstream as many ESE students as possible
   B. Guidance on how to handle ESE students from the ESE teacher
   C. Mutual empowerment of both the mainstream and the ESE teacher
   D. Document progress of mainstreamed students

92. Knowledge of evaluation strategies, program interventions, and types of data are examples of which variable for a successful consultation program?
(Average Rigor) (Skill 3.6)

   A. People
   B. Process
   C. Procedural implementation
   D. Academic preparation

93. Skills as an administrator and background in client, consulter, and consultation skills are examples of which variable in a successful consultation program?
(Average Rigor) (Skill 3.6)

   A. People
   B. Process
   C. Procedural implementation
   D. Academic preparation

94. The ability to identify problems, generate solutions, and knowledge of theoretical perspectives of consultation are examples of which variable in a successful consultation program?
(Average Rigor) (Skill 3.6)

   A. People
   B. Process
   C. Procedural implementation
   D. Academic preparation

95. A serious hindrance to successful mainstreaming is:
(Average Rigor) (Skill 3.6)

   A. Lack of adapted materials
   B. Lack of funding
   C. Lack of communication among teachers
   D. Lack of support from administration

96. Ms. Taylor takes her students to a special gymnastics presentation that the P.E. coach has arranged in the gym. She has a rule against talk-outs and reminds the students that they will lose 5 points on their daily point sheet for talking out. The students get a chance to perform some of the simple stunts. They all easily go through the movements except for Sam, who is known as the class klutz. Sam does not give up, and he finally completes the stunts. His classmates cheer him on with comments like, "Way to go!" Their teacher, however, reminds them that they broke the no-talking rule and will lose the points. What mistake was made here?
(Average Rigor) (Skill 3.6)

    A. The students forgot the no-talking rule.
    B. The teacher considered talk-outs to be maladaptive in all school settings.
    C. The other students could have distracted Sam with talk-outs and caused him to get hurt.
    D. The teacher should have let the P.E. coach handle the discipline in the gym.

97. A student on medication may have his/her dosage adjusted as his/her body grows. Parents may call and ask questions about their child's adjustment to the medication during the school day. During this time you should:
(Average Rigor) (Skill 3.6)

    A. Observe the student for changes in behavior.
    B. Watch for a progression of changed behavior.
    C. Communicate with the parent concerns about sleepiness.
    D. All of the above.

98. You are having continual difficulty with your classroom assistant. A good strategy to address this problem would be:
(Rigorous) (Skill 3.6)

    A. To address the issue immediately
    B. To take away responsibilities
    C. To write a clearly-established role plan to discuss
    D. To speak to your supervisor

99. A consultant teacher should be meeting the needs of his/her students by:
(Easy) (Skill 3.6)

    A. Pushing in to do small group instruction with regular education students
    B. Asking the student to show his/her reasoning for failing
    C. Meeting with the teacher before class to discuss adaptations and expectations
    D. Accompanying the student to class

100. Parent contact should first begin when:
(Average Rigor) (Skill 3.6)

    A. You are informed the child will be your student.
    B. The student fails a test.
    C. The student exceeds others on a task.
    D. A CSE is coming, and you have had no previous replies to letters.

101. Parents of children with disabilities may seek your advice on several aspects regarding their child. A mother calls you and complains she can't keep her son on task so much that she has to keep sending her son back to the bathroom until he finishes getting prepared for the day. What advice should you give her?
(Average Rigor) (Skill 3.6)

    A. Request an educational evaluation.
    B. Recommend close supervision until he does all tasks together consistently.
    C. Create a list of tasks to be completed in the bathroom.
    D. Ask for outside coordination of services advocacy that can assist with this type of issue.

102. Which of the following is NOT an appropriate assessment modification or accommodation for a student with a learning disability?
    (Average Rigor) (Skill 3.7)

    A. Having the test read orally to the student
    B. Writing down the student's dictated answers
    C. Allowing the student to take the assessment home to complete
    D. Extending the time for the student to take the assessment

103. Which of the following is NOT one of the four interrelated components of positive behavioral interventions and supports (PBS)?
    (Rigorous) (Skill 4.1)

    A. Systems change activities
    B. Environmental alterations activities
    C. Behavioral consequences activities
    D. Support provision activities

104. Examples of behaviors that are appropriate to be monitored by measuring duration include all EXCEPT:
    (Average Rigor) (Skill 4.2)

    A. Thumb-sucking
    B. Hitting
    C. Temper tantrums
    D. Maintaining eye contact

105. Examples of behaviors that are appropriate to be monitored by measuring frequency include all EXCEPT:
    (Average Rigor) (Skill 4.2)

    A. Teasing
    B. Talking out
    C. Being on time for class
    D. Off task behavior

106. Criteria for choosing behaviors to measure by frequency include all but those that:
    (Easy) (Skill 4.2)

    A. Have an observable beginning
    B. Last a long time
    C. Last a short time
    D. Occur often

107. Criteria for choosing behaviors to measure by duration include all but those that:
    (Easy) (Skill 4.2)

    A. Last a short time
    B. Last a long time
    C. Have no readily observable beginning or end
    D. Do not happen often

108. Data on quiet behaviors (e.g., nail biting or daydreaming) are best measured using a/an:
    (Rigorous) (Skill 4.2)

    A. Interval or time sample
    B. Continuous sample
    C. Variable sample
    D. Fixed-ratio sample

109. Mr. Jones wants to design an intervention for reducing Jason's sarcastic remarks. He wants to find out who or what is reinforcing Jason's remarks, so he records data on Jason's behavior, as well as the attending behavior of his peers. This is an example of collecting data on:
    (Rigorous) (Skill 4.2)

    A. Reciprocal behaviors
    B. Multiple behaviors for single subjects
    C. Single behaviors for multiple subjects
    D. Qualitative data on Jason

110. Ms. Beekman has a class of students who frequently talk out. She wishes to begin interventions with the students who are talking out the most. She monitors the talking behavior of the entire class for 1-minute samples every half hour. This is an example of collecting data on:
    (Rigorous) (Skill 4.2)

    A. Multiple behaviors for single subjects
    B. Reciprocal behaviors
    C. Single behaviors for multiple subjects
    D. Continuous behaviors for fixed intervals

111. Statements like, "Darren is lazy," are not helpful in describing his behavior for all but which of these reasons?
    (Rigorous) (Skill 4.2)

    A. There is no way to determine if any change occurs from the information given.
    B. The student and not the behavior becomes labeled.
    C. Darren's behavior will manifest itself clearly enough without any written description.
    D. Constructs are open to various interpretations among the people who are asked to define them.

112. Marcie often is not in her seat when the bell rings. She may be found at the pencil sharpener, throwing paper away, or fumbling through her notebook. Which of these descriptions of her behavior can be described as a pinpoint?
    (Average Rigor) (Skill 4.2)

    A. Is tardy a lot
    B. Is out of seat
    C. Is not in seat when the late bell rings
    D. Is disorganized

113. Which of the following should be avoided when writing objectives for social behavior?
    (Easy) (Skill 4.2)

    A. Nonspecific adverbs
    B. Behaviors stated as verbs
    C. Criteria for acceptable performance
    D. Conditions where the behavior is expected to be performed

114. Criteria for choosing behaviors that are in the most need of change involve all but the following:
    (Average Rigor) (Skill 4.2)

    A. Observations across settings to rule out certain interventions
    B. Pinpointing the behavior that is the poorest fit in the child's environment
    C. The teacher's concern about what is the most important behavior to target
    D. Analysis of the environmental reinforcers

115. Anecdotal records should:
    (Average Rigor) (Skill 4.2)

    A. Record observable behavior
    B. End with conjecture
    C. Record motivational factors
    D. Note previously-stated interests

116. Mr. Brown finds that his chosen consequence does not seem to be having the desired effect of reducing the target misbehavior. Which of these would LEAST LIKELY account for Mr. Brown's lack of success with the consequence? *(Average Rigor) (Skill 4.3)*

    A. The consequence was aversive in Mr. Brown's opinion but not the students'.
    B. The students were not developmentally ready to understand the connection between the behavior and the consequence.
    C. Mr. Brown was inconsistent in applying the consequence.
    D. The intervention had not previously been shown to be effective in studies.

117. Which of the following is NOT a feature of effective classroom rules? *(Easy) (Skill 4.3)*

    A. They are about 4 to 6 in number.
    B. They are negatively stated.
    C. Consequences for infractions are consistent and immediate.
    D. They can be tailored to individual classroom goals and teaching styles.

118. Ms. Wright is planning an analysis of Audrey's out-of-seat behavior. Her initial data would be called: *(Rigorous) (Skill 4.3)*

    A. Pre-referral phase
    B. Intervention phase
    C. Baseline phase
    D. Observation phase

119. To reinforce Audrey each time she is on-task and in her seat, Ms. Wright decides to deliver specific praise and stickers, which Audrey may collect and redeem for a reward. The data collected during the time Ms. Wright is using this intervention is called: *(Easy) (Skill 4.3)*

    A. Referral phase
    B. Intervention phase
    C. Baseline phase
    D. Observation phase

120. Crisis intervention methods are concerned above all with: *(Easy) (Skill 4.4)*

    A. Safety and well-being of the staff and students
    B. Stopping the inappropriate behavior
    C. Preventing the behavior from occurring again
    D. The student learning that outbursts are inappropriate

121. Ricky, a third-grade student, runs out of the classroom and onto the roof of the school. He paces around the roof, looks around to see who is watching, and laughs at the people on the ground. He appears to be in control of his behavior. What should the teacher do?
(Average Rigor) (Skill 4.4)

A. Go back inside and leave him up there until he decides he is ready to come down.
B. Climb up to get Ricky so he doesn't fall off and get hurt.
C. Notify the crisis teacher and arrange to have someone monitor Ricky.
D. Call the police.

122. Mr. Smith is on a field trip with a group of high school EH students. On the way, they stop at a fast food restaurant for lunch, and Warren and Raul get into a disagreement. After some heated words, Warren stalks out of the restaurant and refuses to return to the group. He leaves the parking lot, continues walking away from the group, and ignores Mr. Smith's directions to come back. What would be the best course of action for Mr. Smith?
(Average Rigor) (Skill 4.4)

A. Leave the group with the class aide and follow Warren to try to talk him into coming back.
B. Wait a little while and see if Warren cools off and returns.
C. Telephone the school and let the crisis teacher notify the police in accordance with school policy.
D. Call the police himself.

123. An effective classroom behavior management plan includes all EXCEPT which of the following?
 (Easy) (Skill 4.4)

   A. Transition procedures for changing activities
   B. Clear consequences for rule infractions
   C. Concise teacher expectations for student behavior
   D. Copies of lesson plans

124. Which of these would be the LEAST effective measure of behavioral disorders?
 (Easy) (Skill 4.4)

   A. Projective test
   B. Ecological assessment
   C. Achievement test
   D. Psychodynamic analysis

125. When a teacher is choosing behaviors to modify, two issues must be considered. What are they?
 (Average Rigor) (Skill 4.4)

   A. The need for the behavior to be performed in public and the culture of acceptance
   B. The culture of the child and society standards regarding the behavior
   C. Evidence that the behavior can be changed and society norms
   D. Standards of the student's community and school rules

126. According to IDEA 2004, a FBA must be:
 (Average Rigor) (Skill 4.4)

   A. Written by the special education administrator
   B. Written by the teacher who has the issue with the student
   C. Written by the primary teacher
   D. Written by a team

127. Which is the least effective of reinforcers in programs for mildly to moderately handicapped learners?
 (Average Rigor) (Skill 4.5)

   A. Tokens
   B. Social
   C. Food
   D. Activity

128. Teacher feedback, task completion, and a sense of pride over mastery or accomplishment of a skill are examples of:
 (Average Rigor) (Skill 4.5)

   A. Extrinsic reinforcers
   B. Behavior modifiers
   C. Intrinsic reinforcers
   D. Positive feedback

129. Social approval, token reinforcers, and rewards, such as pencils or stickers, are examples of:
 (Average Rigor) (Skill 4.5)

   A. Extrinsic reinforcers
   B. Behavior modifiers
   C. Intrinsic reinforcers
   D. Positive feedback

130. **Token systems are popular for all of these advantages EXCEPT:**
    (Average Rigor) (Skill 4.5)

    A. The number needed for rewards may be adjusted as needed.
    B. Rewards are easy to maintain.
    C. They are effective for students who generally do not respond to social reinforcers.
    D. Tokens reinforce the relationship of desirable behavior and reinforcement.

131. **Skilled readers use all EXCEPT which one of these knowledge sources to construct meanings beyond the literal text:**
    (Rigorous) (Skill 5.1)

    A. Text knowledge
    B. Syntactic knowledge
    C. Morphological knowledge
    D. Semantic knowledge

132. **Indirect requests and attempts to influence or control others through one's use of language is an example of:**
    (Rigorous) (Skill 5.1)

    A. Morphology
    B. Syntax
    C. Pragmatics
    D. Semantics

133. **Kenny, a fourth grader, has trouble comprehending analogies, using comparative, spatial, and temporal words, and multiple meanings. Language interventions for Kenny would focus on:**
    (Rigorous) (Skill 5.1)

    A. Morphology
    B. Syntax
    C. Pragmatics
    D. Semantics

134. **Celia, who is in fourth grade, asked, "Where are my ball?" She also has trouble with passive sentences. Language interventions for Celia would target:**
    (Rigorous) (Skill 5.1)

    A. Morphology
    B. Syntax
    C. Pragmatics
    D. Semantics

135. **Scott is in middle school but still says statements like, "I gotted new high-tops yesterday," and "I saw three mans in the front office." Language interventions for Scott would target:**
    (Average Rigor) (Skill 5.1)

    A. Morphology
    B. Syntax
    C. Pragmatics
    D. Semantics

136. Mark is a 6th grader. You have noticed that he doesn't respond to simple requests like the other students in your class. If you ask him to erase the board, he may look at you, shake his head and say no, but then he will clean the board. When the children gather together for recess, he joins them. Yet, you observe that it takes him much longer to understand the rules to a game. Mark retains what he reads. Mark most likely has:
(Rigorous) (Skill 5.1)

   A. Autism
   B. Tourette's syndrome
   C. Mental retardation
   D. A pragmatic language disability

137. Which of the following is an effective method of gaining and holding students' attention if they are deficient in attending skills?
(Average Rigor) (Skill5.2)

   A. Eliminating or reducing environmental distractions
   B. Asking the question before calling the name of a student to create greater interest
   C. Being enthusiastic and keeping lessons short and interactive
   D. All of the above

138. Task-related attending skills include:
(Rigorous) (Skill 5.2)

   A. Compliance to requests
   B. Writing the correct answer on the chalkboard
   C. Listening to the assignment
   D. Repeating instructions

139. The single most important activity for eventual reading success of young children is:
(Average Rigor) (Skill 5.3)

   A. Giving them books
   B. Watching animated stories
   C. Reading aloud to them
   D. Talking about pictures in books

140. When a student begins to use assistive technology, it is important for the teacher to have a clear outline as to when and how the equipment should be used. Why?
(Rigorous) (Skill 5.4)

   A. To establish a level of accountability with the student
   B. To establish that the teacher has responsibility of the equipment that is in use in his/her room
   C. To establish that the teacher is responsible for the usage of the assistive technology
   D. To establish a guideline for evaluation

141. Sam is working to earn half an hour of basketball time with his favorite P.E. teacher. At the end of each half hour, Sam marks his point sheet with an X if he reached his goal of no call-outs. When he has received 25 marks, he will receive his basketball free time. This behavior management strategy is an example of:
(Average Rigor) (Skill 6.1)

    A. Self-recording
    B. Self-evaluation
    C. Self-reinforcement
    D. Self-regulation

142. Mark has been working on his target goal of completing his mathematics class work. Each day, he records, on a scale of 0 to 3, how well he has done his work, and his teacher provides feedback. This self-management technique is an example of:
(Average Rigor) (Skill 6.1)

    A Self-recording
    B. Self-reinforcement
    C. Self-regulation
    D. Self-evaluation

143. When Barbara reached her target goal, she chose her reinforcer and softly said to herself, "I worked hard, and I deserve this reward." This self-management technique is an example of:
(Average Rigor) (Skill 6.1)

    A. Self-reinforcement
    B. Self-recording
    C. Self-regulation
    D. Self-evaluation

144. Teaching children functional skills that will be useful in their home life and neighborhoods is the basis of:
(Rigorous) (Skill 6.1)

    A. Curriculum-based instruction
    B. Community-based instruction
    C. Transition planning
    D. Functional curriculum

145. Measurement of adaptive behavior should include all EXCEPT:
(Rigorous) (Skill 6.1)

    A. Student's behavior in a variety of settings
    B. Student's skills displayed in a variety of settings
    C. Comparative analysis to other students in his/her class
    D. Analysis of student's social skills

146. **Functional curriculum focuses on all of the following EXCEPT:**
    (Rigorous) (Skill 6.1)

    A. Skills needed for social living
    B. Occupational readiness
    C. Functioning in society
    D. Remedial academic skills

147. **In order to effectively differentiate instruction, the teacher must do all of the following EXCEPT:**
    (Average Rigor) (Skill 3.5)

    A. Assess where individual students are with reference to an objective
    B. Design some lesson material that addresses the objective at a cognitively less demanding level
    C. Assess all students uniformly, on the same set of standards
    D. Design some lesson material that addresses the objective on a more advanced level

148. **A student with a poor self-concept may manifest in all of the ways listed below EXCEPT:**
    (Average Rigor) (Skill 6.3)

    A. Withdrawn actions
    B. Aggression
    C. Consistently announcing his/her achievements
    D. Shyness

149. **Career exploration involves all of the following activities EXCEPT:**
    (Rigorous) (Skill 7.1)

    A. Listening to guest speakers
    B. Contextual learning activities
    C. Simulated work experiences
    D. Job shadowing

150. **The transition activities that have to be addressed, unless the IEP team finds it uncalled for, include all of the following EXCEPT:**
    (Rigorous) (Skill 7.2)

    A. Instruction
    B. Volunteer opportunities
    C. Community experiences
    D. Development of objectives related to employment and other post-school areas

Answer Key: Post-test

1.	B	45.	A	89.	D	133.	D
2.	A	46.	C	90.	D	134.	B
3.	C	47.	C	91.	C	135.	A
4.	A	48.	A	92.	B	136.	D
5.	C	49.	B	93.	A	137.	D
6.	A	50.	B	94.	C	138.	C
7.	B	51.	D	95.	C	139.	C
8.	D	52.	C	96.	D	140.	A
9.	B	53.	C	97.	D	141.	A
10.	B	54.	D	98.	C	142.	D
11.	D	55.	B	99.	A	143.	A
12.	B	56.	A	100.	A	144.	B
13.	B	57.	C	101.	C	145.	C
14.	A	58.	B	102.	C	146.	D
15.	C	59.	C	103.	D	147.	C
16.	D	60.	A	104.	B	148.	C
17.	D	61.	C	105.	D	149.	A
18.	A	62.	B	106.	B	150.	B
19.	D	63.	C	107.	A		
20.	A	64.	D	108.	A		
21.	D	65.	C	109.	A		
22.	A	66.	C	110.	C		
23.	A	67.	C	111.	C		
24.	D	68.	C	112.	C		
25.	A	69.	B	113.	A		
26.	D	70.	C	114.	C		
27.	C	71.	C	115.	A		
28.	B	72.	C	116.	D		
29.	D	73.	D	117.	B		
30.	C	74.	C	118.	C		
31.	B	75.	C	119.	B		
32.	A	76.	B	120.	A		
33.	B	77.	A	121.	C		
34.	B	78.	D	122.	C		
35.	B	79.	C	123.	D		
36.	C	80.	C	124.	C		
37.	A	81.	B	125.	B		
38.	D	82.	B	126.	D		
39.	B	83.	C	127.	C		
40.	C	84.	A	128.	C		
41.	C	85.	C	129.	A		
42.	C	86.	C	130.	B		
43.	A	87.	B	131.	C		
44.	C	88.	C	132.	C		

Rigor Table: Post-test

	Easy %20	Average Rigor %40	Rigorous %40
Question #	5, 6, 8, 11, 12, 14, 21, 24, 26, 32, 36, 43, 44, 50, 55, 59, 62, 63, 64, 67, 72, 91, 99, 106, 107, 113, 117, 119, 120, 123, 124	1, 2, 7, 10, 13, 23, 25, 28, 29, 30, 31, 33, 41, 45, 47, 48, 53, 56, 57, 61, 65, 68, 73, 74, 81, 83, 85, 86, 88, 89, 90, 92, 93, 94, 95, 96, 97, 100, 101, 102, 104, 105, 112, 114, 115, 116, 121, 122, 125, 126, 127, 128, 129, 130, 135, 137, 139, 141, 142, 143, 148	3, 4, 9, 15, 16, 17, 18, 19, 20, 22, 27, 34, 35, 37, 38, 39, 40, 42, 46, 49, 51, 52, 54, 58, 60, 66, 69, 70, 71, 75, 76, 77, 78, 79, 80, 82, 84, 87, 98, 103, 108, 109, 110, 111, 118, 131, 132, 133, 134, 136, 138, 140, 144, 145, 146, 147, 149, 150

Rationales with Sample Questions: Post-test

1. **The minimum number of IEP meetings required per year is:** *(Average Rigor) (Skill 1.1)*

    A. As many as necessary
    B. One
    C. Two
    D. Three

Answer: B. One

P. L. 99-457 (1986) grants an annual IEP.

2. **Which of these groups is not comprehensively covered by IDEA?** *(Average Rigor) (Skill 1.1)*

    A. Gifted and talented
    B. Mentally retarded
    C. Specific learning disabilities
    D. Speech and language impaired

Answer: A. Gifted and talented

The Individuals with Disabilities Education Act, 101-476 (1990), did not cover all exceptional children. It did not address the needs of gifted students. The Gifted and Talented Children's Act, P. L. 95-56, was passed in 1978.

3. **Educators who advocate educating all children in their neighborhood classrooms and schools, who propose the end of labeling and segregation of special needs students in special classes, and who call for the delivery of special supports and services directly in the classroom, may be said to support the:** *(Rigorous) (Skill 1.7)*

    A. Full service model
    B. Regular education initiative
    C. Full inclusion model
    D. Mainstream model

Answer: C. Full inclusion model

Advocates of the full inclusion model believe all students must be included in the regular classroom.

4. Section 504 differs from the scope of IDEA because its main focus is on:
   (Rigorous) (Skill 1.1)

   A. Prohibition of discrimination on the basis of disability
   B. A basis for additional support services and accommodations in a special education setting
   C. Procedural rights and safeguards for the individual
   D. Federal funding for educational services

Answer: A. Prohibition of discrimination on the basis of disability

Section 504 prohibits discrimination on the basis of disability.

5. Public Law 99-457 amended the EHA to make provisions for:
   (Easy) (Skill 1.1)

   A. Education services for "uneducable" children
   B. Education services for children in jail settings
   C. Special education benefits for children birth to five years
   D. Education services for medically-fragile children

Answer: C. Special education benefits for children birth to five years

P.L. 99-457 amended EHA to provide special education programs for children 3-5 years, with most states offering outreach programs to identify children with special needs from birth to age 3.

6. Under the provisions of IDEA, the student is entitled to all of these EXCEPT:
   (Easy) (Skill 1.1)

   A. Placement in the best environment
   B. Placement in the least restrictive environment
   C. Provision of educational needs at no cost
   D. Provision of individualized, appropriate educational program

Answer: A. Placement in the best environment

IDEA mandates a least restrictive environment, an IEP (individual education plan), and a free public education.

TEACHER CERTIFICATION STUDY GUIDE

7. **Students who can recognize and name some letters and apply sounds to many of the consonants, and can do some invented spelling, but do not recognize common spelling patterns are in which phase of learning to decode?**

    A. Pre-alphabetic phase
    B. Partial alphabetic phase
    C. Full- alphabetic phase
    D. Consolidated alphabetic phase

Answer: B. partial alphabetic phase

Ehri's five stages of alphabetic knowledge are:
1. **Pre-alphabetic phase**: Children respond to words as visual gestalts in context by memorizing their visual features, but don't yet understand phoneme/letter correspondence. They might recognize the word "stop" inside the usual hexagon shaped sign, but not recognize it in connected text.
2. **Partial-alphabetic phase:** Children can name some letters of the alphabet, apply sounds to many of the consonants. They can identify more words in different contexts, but cannot handle vowel sounds well and don't recognize common spelling patterns.
3. **Full-alphabetic phase:** Children have a good understanding of the graphophonemic system and fully grasp the connection between graphemes and phonemes. They can decode letter by letter and spell phonetically. They can decode unfamiliar words and store sight words in memory.
4. **Consolidated-alphabetic phase:** Children tend to see words as whole units and use all their decoding skills in unison to decode unfamiliar words, allowing them to decode multi-syllable words and decode words by analogy. At this stage they can also use such things as prefixes and suffixes as clues to decoding new words.
5. **Automatic phase:** At this phase, the child's decoding has reached a state of automaticity where word-level reading predominates, and reading is fluent and comprehension rivals that of listening comprehension.

8. **The following words all describe an IEP objective EXCEPT:**
    (Easy) (Skill 1.1)

    A. Specific
    B. Observable
    C. Measurable
    D. Criterion-referenced

Answer: D. Criterion-referenced

An Individual Education Plan should be specific, observable, and measurable.

TEACHER CERTIFICATION STUDY GUIDE

9. Which of the following statements was not offered as a rationale for Regular Education Intervention (REI) or Inclusion?
   (Rigorous) (Skill 1.1)

   A. Special education students are not usually identified until their learning problems have become severe.
   B. Lack of funding will mean that support for the special needs children will not be available in the regular classroom.
   C. Putting children in segregated special education placements is stigmatizing.
   D. There are students with learning or behavior problems who do not meet special education requirements but who still need special services.

Answer: B. Lack of funding will mean that support for special needs children will not be available in the regular classroom.

All except lack of funding were offered in support of Regular Education Intervention or Inclusion.

10. Hector is a 10th grader in a program for the severely emotionally handicapped. After a classmate taunted him about his mother, Hector threw a desk at the other boy and attacked him. As a crisis intervention team tried to break up the fight, one teacher hurt his knee. The other boy received a concussion. Hector now faces disciplinary measures. How long can he be suspended without the suspension constituting a "change of placement"?
    (Average Rigor) (Skill 1.1)

    A. 5 days
    B. 10 days
    C. 10 + 30 days
    D. 60 days

Answer: B. 10 days

According to *Honig versus Doe,* 1988, where the student has presented an immediate threat to others, that student may be temporarily suspended for up to 10 school days to give the school and the parents time to review the IEP and discuss possible alternatives to the current placement.

TEACHER CERTIFICATION STUDY GUIDE

11. The concept that a handicapped student cannot be expelled for misconduct that is a manifestation of the handicap itself is not limited to students who are labeled "seriously emotionally disturbed." Which reason does NOT explain this concept? *(Easy) (Skill 1.1)*

    A. Emphasis on individualized evaluation.
    B. Consideration of the problems and needs of handicapped students.
    C. Right to a free and appropriate public education.
    D. Putting these students out of school will just leave them on the streets to commit crimes.

Answer: D. Putting these students out of school will just leave them on the streets to commit crimes.

A, B, and C are tenets of IDEA and should take place in the least restrictive environment. D does not explain this concept.

12. Jonathan has Attention Deficit Hyperactivity Disorder (ADHD). He is in a regular classroom and appears to be doing okay. However, his teacher does not want John in her class because he will not obey her when she asks him to stop doing a repetitive action such as tapping his foot. The teacher sees this as distracting during tests. John needs: *(Easy) (Skill 1.1)*

    A. An IEP
    B. A 504 Plan
    C. A VESID evaluation
    D. A more restrictive environment

Answer: B. A 504 Plan

John is exhibiting normal grade level behavior with the exception of the ADHD behaviors, which may need some acceptance for his academic success. John has not shown any academic deficiencies. John needs a 504 Plan to provide small adaptations to meet his needs. These would be accommodations that would allow alternative behaviors that would meet his ADHD needs without distracting his classmates (e.g., wiggle seat, pillow or sponge to tap on, other "fiddle objects).

13. **IDEA 2004 states that there is a disproportionate number of minority students classified as needing special education services. IDEA 2004 suggests this is due to:**
  (Average Rigor) (Skill 1.1)

    A. Socioeconomic status where disproportionate numbers exist
    B. Improper evaluations – Not making allowances for students who have English as a second language
    C. Growing population of minorities
    D. Percentage of drug abuse per ethnicity

Answer: B. Improper evaluations – Not making allowances for students who have English as a second language

IDEA 2004 questioned the acceptance or inclusion of students who have English as a second language as being over represented. The fact that a child's native language is not English is not a disability.

14. **NCLB and IDEA 2004 changed special education teacher requirements by:** *(Easy) (Skill 1.1)*

    A. Requiring a highly-qualified status for job placement
    B. Adding changes to the requirement for certifications
    C. Adding legislation requiring teachers to maintain knowledge of law
    D. Requiring inclusive environmental experience prior to certification

Answer: A. Requiring a highly-qualified status for job placement

NCLB and IDEA 2004 place a requirement that all teachers shall be equally qualified to teach in their content areas.

TEACHER CERTIFICATION STUDY GUIDE

15. Which law specifically states that, "Full Inclusion is not the only way for a student to reach his/her highest potential"?
    (Rigorous) (Skill 1.1)

    A. IDEA
    B. IDEA 97
    C. IDEA 2004
    D. Part 200

Answer: C. IDEA 2004

In IDEIAA (IDEA 2004), stated that full inclusion was not always best for the individual student. A small number of students may need much smaller group instruction, highly specialized or extensive instruction techniques, or a more protected environment. For such students, a smaller, substantially separate class may be "least restrictive" *for them*. This allows students who need a different setting in order to learn to be served appropriately in a more "restrictive" setting when people who push full inclusion are confronted. Of course, it is necessary in such situations to attend to the child's social needs and ensure that the child is included with peers to the greatest extent possible given the specific disabilities and needs involved.

16. NCLB (No Child Left Behind Act) was signed on January 8, 2002. It addresses what? *(Rigorous) (Skill 1.1)*

    A. Accessibility of curriculum to the student
    B. Administrative incentives for school improvements
    C. The funding to provide services required
    D. Accountability of school personnel for student achievement

Answer: D. Accountability of school personnel for student achievement

School personnel are responsible for teaching grade appropriate curriculum goals with modifications and accommodations for students' disabilities and special needs. This may require using entry level objectives or alternative assessment methods, as well.

TEACHER CERTIFICATION STUDY GUIDE

17. **IDEA 97 changed IDEA by requiring:**
    (Rigorous) (Skill 1.1)

    A. IEPs to be in electronic format
    B. Requiring all staff working with the student to have access to the IEP
    C. Allowing past assessments to be used in Triennials
    D. BIPs for many students with FBAs

Answer: D. BIPs for many students with FBAs

IDEA 97 created a mandate to provide interventions to change inappropriate behaviors to increase the possibility that the student could avoid the consequences of repeating the behavior.

18. **What legislation started FAPE?**
    (Rigorous) (Skill 1.1)

    A. Section 504
    B. EHCA
    C. IDEA
    D. Education Amendment 1974

Answer: A. Section 504

FAPE stands for Free Appropriate Public Education. Section 504 of the Rehabilitation Act in 1973 is the legislation that enacted/created FAPE.

TEACHER CERTIFICATION STUDY GUIDE

19. According to the National Reading Panel, which of the following activities would NOT be a best practice for increasing phoneme awareness?
    (Average) (Skill 5.11)

    A. Oral rhyming games
    B. Matching oral words based on the beginning, middle, or ending sound.
    C. Singing songs like "Knick, Knack, Paddy Whack" where single sounds are rearranged or changed
    D. Using letter tiles to spell out simple words

Answer: D. Using letter tiles to spell out simple words

Using letters turns this into a *phonics* task, not a *phoneme awareness* task. Phoneme awareness is one part of phonological awareness, and is the understanding that spoken words are composed of tiny, individual sound units, called phonemes.

The key in phonemic awareness is that it can be taught with the students' eyes closed. In other words, it's all about sounds, not about ascribing written letters to sounds. To be phonemically aware means that the reader and listener can recognize and manipulate specific sounds in **spoken** words. Phonemic awareness deals with sounds in words that are spoken. The majority of phonemic awareness tasks, activities, and exercises are therefore ORAL.

20. The revision of Individuals with Disabilities Education Act in 1997 required:
    (Rigorous) (Skill 1.1)

    A. Collaboration of educational professionals in order to provide equitable opportunities for students with disabilities.
    B. Removed the requirement for short-term objectives for objectives with goals.
    C. School administrator approval for an IEP to be put into place.
    D. FBAs and BIPs for all students who were suspended for 6 days.

Answer: A. Collaboration of educational professionals in order to provide equitable opportunities for students with disabilities.

Teachers must collaborate professionally to render the best possible education to the student.

TEACHER CERTIFICATION STUDY GUIDE

21. **A person who has a learning disability has:**
    (Easy) (Skill 1.1)

    A. An IQ two standard deviations below the norm
    B. Congenital abnormalities
    C. Is limited by the educational environment
    D. Has a disorder in one of the basic psychological processes

Answer: D. Has a disorder in one of the basic psychological processes

The definition of "learning disability" begins: a disorder in one or more of the basic psychological processes involved in understanding or in using language, spoken or written.

22. **IDEA 2004 changed the IEP by?**
    (Rigorous) (Skill 1.1)

    A. Not requiring short-term objectives
    B. Requiring an inclusive activity
    C. Requiring parents to participate in the CSE
    D. Establishing new criteria to be classified as learning disabled

Answer: A. Not requiring short-term objectives

Until IDEA 2004, short term goals/objectives needed to be in place to see progress towards a goal.

23. **According to IDEA 2004, students with disabilities are to do what?**
    (Average) (Skill 1.1)

    A. Participate in the general education program to the fullest extent that it is beneficial for them
    B. Participate in a vocational training within the general education setting
    C. Participate in a general education setting for physical education
    D. Participate in a modified program that meets his/her needs

Answer: A. Participate in the general education program to the fullest extent that it is beneficial for them

B, C, and D are all possible settings related to participating in the general education setting to the fullest extent possible. This still can mean that a student's LRE may restrict him/her to a 12:1:1 for the entire school day.

TEACHER CERTIFICATION STUDY GUIDE

24. **Satisfaction of the LRE requirement means:**
    (Easy) (Skill 1.2)

    A. The school is providing the best services it can offer.
    B. The school is providing the best services the district has to offer.
    C. The student is being educated with the fewest special education services necessary.
    D. The student is being educated in the least restrictive setting that meets his or her needs.

Answer: D. The student is being educated in the least restrictive setting that meets his or her needs.

The legislation mandates LRE (Least Restrictive Environment). The specifics of what environment constitutes "least restrictive" will vary depending upon each child's needs.

25. **A review of a student's eligibility for an exceptional student program must be done:**
    (Average Rigor) (Skill 1.2)

    A. At least once every three years
    B. At least once a year
    C. Only if a major change occurs in academic or behavioral performance
    D. When a student transfers to a new school

Answer: A. At least once every three years

The reauthorization of IDEA 2004 requires reevaluation must occur at least once every three years, but not more often than once a year, unless the parent and the school agree it is unnecessary.

TEACHER CERTIFICATION STUDY GUIDE

26. Which of the following would be effective techniques for improving fluency?
    (Easy Rigor) (Skill 5.13)

    A. Choral reading
    B. Reader's theatre
    C. Modeling and recorded books
    D. All of the above

Answer: D. All of the above.

All of these, as well as paired reading, frequent independent reading, repeated reading aloud of the same passage, and drilling on high frequency sight words, have been shown to be helpful in improving fluency and prosody.

27. Lack of regular follow-up, difficulty in transporting materials, and lack of consistent support for students who need more assistance are disadvantages of which type of service model?
    (Rigorous) (Skill 1.2)

    A. Regular classroom
    B. Consultant with regular teacher
    C. Itinerant
    D. Resource room

Answer: C. Itinerant

The itinerant model, as the name implies, is not regular. It requires the specialist to move from school to school on an irregular basis.

TEACHER CERTIFICATION STUDY GUIDE

28. Ability to supply specific instructional materials, programs, and methods and to influence environmental learning variables on a regular basis in a mainstream classroom are advantages of which service model for exceptional students?
    (Average Rigor) (Skill 1.2)

    A. Regular classroom
    B. Consultant teacher
    C. Itinerant teacher
    D. Resource room

Answer: B. Consultant teacher

Consultation is usually done by specialists, who provide services (direct and/or indirect) to students who attend general education classes on a full-time basis and/or to such students' general education teacher.

29. An emphasis on instructional remediation and individualized instruction in problem areas, and a focus on mainstreaming students in areas that are not a problem, are characteristics of which model of service delivery?
    (Average Rigor) (Skill 1.2)

    A. Regular classroom
    B. Consultant teacher
    C. Itinerant teacher
    D. Resource room

Answer: D. Resource room

The resource room is usually a bridge to mainstreaming. The student is in the resource room only for the subject(s) that cause great difficulty.

30. Which of these would not be considered a valid attempt to contact a parent for an IEP meeting?
    (Average Rigor) (Skill 1.2)

    A. Telephone call
    B. Copy of correspondence
    C. Message left on answering machine
    D. Record of home visits

Answer: C. Message left on answering machine

A message left on an answering machine is not direct contact.

31. Cheryl is a 15-year old student receiving educational services in a full-time EH classroom. The date for her IEP review is planned for two months before her 16th birthday. According to the requirements of IDEA, what must ADDITIONALLY be included in this review?
    (Average Rigor) (Skill 1.2)

    A. Graduation plan
    B. Individualized transition plan
    C. Individualized family service plan
    D. Transportation planning

Answer: B. Individualized transition plan

This is necessary, as the student should be transitioning from school to work.

TEACHER CERTIFICATION STUDY GUIDE

32. **Most students with disabilities develop better self-images and recognize their own academic and social strengths when they are:** *(Easy) (Skill 1.2)*

    A. Included in the mainstream classroom
    B. Provided community-based internships
    C. Socializing in the hallway
    D. Provided 1:1 instructional opportunity

Answer: A. Included in the mainstream classroom

When a child with a disability is included in the regular classroom, it raises the expectations of the child's academic performance and his or her need to conform to "acceptable peer behavior." In order for this to be true, however, the child must be *capable* of meeting these behavioral and learning standards *in that setting*. The new IDEA recognizes that this is not true for all children. It is important not to "set a child up for failure" by assuming that all children can meet the same standard or learn in the same setting. It is also necessary for the student to be accepted by peers and this may require the school staff to work with the general education population to be sure *they* have the attitudes and the interpersonal skills to make all children feel welcome and included. It is not enough to just thrust a student with special needs into the mainstream and assume that all will be well. It is important to provide the scaffolding necessary to all students and staff to help make such inclusion successful.

TEACHER CERTIFICATION STUDY GUIDE

33. **A best practice for evaluating student performance and progress on IEPs is:**
    (Average Rigor) (Skill 2.3)

    A. Standardized assessment
    B. Criterion-based assessment
    C. Rating scales
    D. Norm-referenced assessment

Answer: B. Criterion-based assessment

Evaluating progress on an IEP requires criterion-based assessment because one is evaluating the extent to which the student has met certain criteria (the goals and objectives in the IEP). Such criterion based assessment can be formal or informal, commercial or teacher designed, as long as it assesses the relevant criteria. Standardized assessments may or may not be criterion based ("standardized" refers to the manner in which the test is administered, not its content). Norm referenced assessments are designed to compare the student to grade or age peers, not whether the student has met certain learning goals. Rating scales are assessments of behavioral or emotional variables, not learning goals.

34. **Guidelines for an Individualized Family Service Plan (IFSP) would be described in which legislation?**
    (Rigorous) (Skill 1.3)

    A. P.L. 94-142 (Education of the Handicapped, 1975)
    B. P.L. 99 – 457 (EHA Revisions, 1986)
    C. P.L. 101 – 476 (Idea reauthorization of EHA, 1990)
    D. ADA (Americans with Disabilities Act, 1990)

Answer: B. P.L. 99 – 457 (EHA Revisions, 1986)

P.L. 99-457, 1986, is a revision of the Education for all Handicapped Children Act and it extends services for children ages 3-5 and their families. P.L. 101 – 476 is IDEA, and is the reauthorization and renaming of EHA). P.L. 94 – 142, Education for All Handicapped Children Act, was passed in the Civil Rights era, and is the original act that provides a free and appropriate education for children with handicaps. ADA is the Americans with Disabilities Act, a form of anti-discrimination legislation passed in 1990.

TEACHER CERTIFICATION STUDY GUIDE

35. Which of these characteristics is NOT included in the P.L. 94-142 definition of emotional disturbance?
    (Rigorous) (Skill 1.4)

    A. General pervasive mood of unhappiness or depression
    B. Social maladjustment manifested in a number of settings
    C. Tendency to develop physical symptoms, pains, or fear associated with school or personal problems
    D. Inability to learn that is not attributed to intellectual, sensory, or health factors

Answer: B. Social maladjustment manifested in a number of settings

Social maladjustment is not considered a disability.

36. Justin is diagnosed with autism and is in an inclusive setting. You were called down to "Stop him from turning the lights off and remove him." When you arrive, you learn that today a movie was supposed to be finished, but the VCR broke, so the teacher planned another activity. What is the best way to explain to the teacher why Justin was turning off the lights?
    (Easy) (Skill 1.4)

    A. He is perseverating and will stop shortly.
    B. He is telling you the lights bother him.
    C. He needs forewarning before a transition. Next time you have an unexpected change in classroom schedule, please let him know.
    D. Please understand that this is part of who Justin is. He will leave the lights alone after I talk to him.

Answer: C. He needs forewarning before a transition. Next time you have an unexpected change in classroom schedule please let him know.

The teacher already knows that Justin will stop after you talk to him. That is why she called you. She needs to know what to do if this happens again. Explaining the problem with transition may enable the teacher to see and plan for a problem before it occurs or to prevent a possible problem.

37. According to IDEA, a child whose disability is related to being deaf and blind may not be classified as:
    (Rigorous) (Skill 1.4)

    A. Multiply Disabled
    B. Other Health Impaired
    C. Mentally Retarded
    D. Visually Impaired

Answer: A. Multiply Disabled

The only stated area where deaf-blindness is not accepted is in Multiple Disabilities. There is a separate category for deaf-blind.

38. A child may be classified under the special education "umbrella" as having Traumatic Brain Injury (TBI) if he/she does not have the following cause?
    (Rigorous) (Skill 1.4)

    A. Stroke
    B. Anoxia
    C. Encephalitis
    D. Birth trauma

Answer: D. Birth trauma

According to IDEA and Part 200, a child may not be labeled as having Traumatic Brain Injury if the injury is related to birth.

39. In mainstream America, which body language would not likely be interpreted as a sign of defensiveness, aggression, or hostility?
    (Rigorous) (Skill 1.5)

    A. Pointing
    B. Direct eye contact
    C. Hands on hips
    D. Arms crossed

Answer: B. Direct eye contact

In mainstream American culture, A, C, and D are considered nonverbal acts of defiance. Direct eye contact is not considered an act of defiance.

TEACHER CERTIFICATION STUDY GUIDE

40. **Of the various factors that contribute to delinquency and anti-social behavior, which has been found to be the weakest?**
    (Rigorous) (Skill 1.5)

    A. Criminal behavior and/or alcoholism in the father
    B. Lax mother and punishing father
    C. Socioeconomic disadvantage
    D. Long history of broken home and marital discord among parents

Answer: C. Socioeconomic disadvantage

There are many examples of A, B, and D where there is socio-economic advantage. Socio-economic disadvantage, in itself, does not cause delinquency.

41. **Poor moral development, lack of empathy, and behavioral excesses, such as aggression, are the most obvious characteristics of which behavioral disorder?**
    (Average Rigor) (Skill 1.5)

    A. Autism
    B. ADHD
    C. Conduct disorder
    D. Pervasive developmental disorder

Answer: C. Conduct disorder

A student with conduct disorder or social maladjustment displays behaviors/values that are in conflict with the school, home, or community. The characteristics listed are all behavioral/social.

TEACHER CERTIFICATION STUDY GUIDE

42. School refusal, obsessive-compulsive disorders, psychosis, and separation anxiety are also frequently accompanied by:
    (Rigorous) (Skill 1.5)

    A. Conduct disorder
    B. ADHD
    C. Depression
    D. Autism

Answer: C. Depression

These behaviors are often accompanied by depression. Depression is one component of many psychological disorders and dignosis of these other disorders must address the possibility of depression, as well. ADHD *can* accompany some of these disorders, but it cannot be assumed a child with ADHD will have these other disorders. In addition, ADHD is very are with psychoses. Conduct disorder is a separate disorder, as is Autism.

43. Signs of depression do not typically include:
    (Easy) (Skill 1.5)

    A. Hyperactivity
    B. Changes in sleep patterns
    C. Recurring thoughts of death or suicide
    D. Significant changes in weight or appetite

Answer: A. Hyperactivity

Depression is usually characterized by listlessness, brooding, low motivation, and little activity. Conversely, hyperactivity is over activity.

44. Children who are characterized by impulsivity generally:
    (Easy) (Skill 1.5)

    A. Do not feel sorry for their actions
    B. Blame others for their actions
    C. Do not weigh alternatives before acting
    D. Do not outgrow their problem

Answer: C. Do not weigh alternatives before acting

They act without thinking, so they either cannot think or do not think before they act.

TEACHER CERTIFICATION STUDY GUIDE

45. **Which of these is listed as only a minor scale on the Behavior Problem Checklist?**
    (Average Rigor) (Skill 1.5)

    A. Motor excess
    B. Conduct disorder
    C. Socialized aggression
    D. Anxiety/withdrawal

Answer: A. Motor excess

Motor excess has to do with over activity, or hyperactivity, in physical movement. The other three items are disorders, all of which may be characterized by excessive activity.

46. **Which of these explanations would not likely account for the lack of a clear definition of behavior disorders?**
    (Rigorous) (Skill 1.5)

    A. Problems with measurement
    B. Cultural and/or social influences and views of what is acceptable
    C. The numerous types of manifestations of behavior disorders
    D. Differing theories that use their own terminology and definitions

Answer: C. The numerous types of manifestations of behavior disorders

A, B, and D are factors that account for the lack of a clear definition of some behavioral disorders. C is not a factor.

47. **Ryan is 3, and her temper tantrums last for an hour. Bryan is 8, and he does not stay on task for more than 10 minutes without teacher prompts. These behaviors differ from normal children in terms of their:**
    (Average Rigor) (Skill 1.5)

    A. Rate
    B. Topography
    C. Duration
    D. Magnitude

Answer: C. Duration

It is not normal for temper tantrums to last an hour. At age eight, a normal student stays on task much longer than ten minutes without teacher prompts.

48. All children cry, hit, fight, and play alone at different times. Children with behavior disorders will perform these behaviors at a higher than normal:
    (Average Rigor) (Skill 1.5)

    A. Rate
    B. Topography
    C. Duration
    D. Magnitude

Answer: A. Rate

Children with behavior disorders display them at a much higher rate than normal children.

49. The exhibition of two or more types of problem behaviors across different areas of functioning is known as:
    (Rigorous) (Skill 1.5)

    A. Multiple maladaptive behaviors
    B. Clustering
    C. Social maladjustment
    D. Conduct disorder

Answer: B. Clustering

Children with behavior disorders sometimes do not display a single behavior. They display a range of behaviors. These behaviors are usually clustered together, hence, clustering.

TEACHER CERTIFICATION STUDY GUIDE

50. Children with behavior disorders often do not exhibit stimulus control. This means they have not learned:
(Easy) (Skill 1.5)

   A. The right things to do
   B. Where and when certain behaviors are appropriate
   C. Right from wrong
   D. Listening skills

Answer: B. Where and when certain behaviors are appropriate

These children respond to stimuli at almost any place and time. They are not able to stop and think about the relevance of the context or control their responses to stimuli. They have not learned that a behavior that is acceptable in one context will not be acceptable in another.

51. Truancy, gang membership, and feelings of pride in belonging to a delinquent subculture are indicative of:
(Rigorous) (Skill 1.5)

   A. Conduct disorder
   B. Personality disorders
   C. Immaturity
   D. Socialized aggression

Answer: D. Socialized aggression

The student is acting out by using aggression. This gives him a sense of belonging.

52. Which of these is not true for most children with behavior disorders?
(Rigorous) (Skill 1.5)

   A. Many score in the "slow learner" or "mildly retarded" range on IQ tests.
   B. They are frequently behind their classmates in academic achievement.
   C. They are bright but bored with their surroundings.
   D. A large amount of time is spent in nonproductive, nonacademic behaviors.

Answer: C. They are bright but bored with their surroundings.

Most children with conduct disorders display the traits found in A, B, and D.

53. Echolalia, repetitive stereotyped actions, and a severe disorder of thinking and communication are indicative of:
    (Average Rigor) (Skill 1.5)

    A. Psychosis
    B. Schizophrenia
    C. Autism
    D. Paranoia

Answer: C. Autism

The behaviors listed are indicative of autism.

54. Which behavioral disorder is difficult to diagnose in children because the symptoms are manifested quite differently than in adults?
    (Rigorous) (Skill 1.5)

    A. Anorexia
    B. Schizophrenia
    C. Paranoia
    D. Depression

Answer: D. Depression

Since a child is less mature cognitively, the child can manifest depression somewhat differently. Children are less adept at verbalizing their feelings, so they may express depression in their behavior. Their depression may be overlooked as moodiness, lack of motivation, or "a stage he's going through." Childhood depression often has a more visible anxiety component, continued irritability, or failure to gain weight. Serious depression in children may involve hallucinations, where similar levels in more cognitively advanced adults may involve full blown delusions.

TEACHER CERTIFICATION STUDY GUIDE

55. Tom's special education teacher became concerned about her ability to deliver the adaptations and services Tom needs when she heard him begin to talk to someone who was not there. Tom also responds to questions in a nonsensical manner. Tom's teacher is concerned because she thinks he may be exhibiting symptoms of:
    (Easy) (Skill 1.5)

    A. Sensory perceptual disorder
    B. Mental illnesses
    C. Depression
    D. Tactile sensory deprivation.

Answer: B. Mental illnesses

Tom is demonstrating delusional or hallucinogenic symptoms. These symptoms may indicate a need for psychiatric treatment within a more restrictive environment.

56. Janice is a new student in your self-contained class. She is extremely quiet and makes little, if any, eye contact. Yesterday, she started to "parrot" what another student said. Today, you became concerned when she did not follow directions and seemed not to even recognize your presence. Her cumulative file arrived today; when you review the health section, it most likely will state that she is diagnosed with:
    (Average Rigor) (Skill 1.5)

    A. Autism
    B. Central Processing Disorder
    C. Traumatic Brain Injury
    D. Mental Retardation

Answer: A. Autism

Janice is exhibiting 3 symptoms of Autism. While a child may demonstrate some of these behaviors, if he or she is diagnosed with Traumatic Brain Injury or Mental Retardation, the combination of these symptoms is more likely to indicate Autism.

TEACHER CERTIFICATION STUDY GUIDE

57. **The National Reading Panel (2000) Report identified all of these as critical areas of reading instruction EXCEPT:**
    (Average Rigor) (Skill 5.9)

    A. Phoneme Awareness
    B. Fluency
    C. Memory
    D. Vocabulary

Answer: C. Memory.

The National Reading Panel reviewed research demonstrating the importance of these five components of any reading program: **Phonemic Awareness**; the understanding that spoken words are made up of individual sounds, one part of overall phonological awareness; **Phonics**; the process of linking sounds to letter symbols and combining them to make words; **Fluency**; the ability to read with speed, accuracy and proper expression; **Vocabulary**; understanding the meaning of individual words in context; and **Comprehension**; the process of getting meaning or information from text which occurs on multiple levels, from literal to abstract. Memory is a basic cognitive capacity that affects all types of learning, but it is not identified as one of the five critical areas of instruction

58. **Which one of the following is NOT a primary purpose of an IEP?**
    (Rigorous) (Skill 1.6)

    A. To outline instructional programs
    B. To develop self-advocacy skills
    C. To function as the basis for evaluation
    D. To facilitate communication among staff members, teachers, parents, and students

Answer: B. To develop self-advocacy skills

While self-advocacy should be encouraged, it is not one of the primary purposes of an IEP.

EXCEP. STUDENT EDU. K-12

TEACHER CERTIFICATION STUDY GUIDE

59. **Kara's mother has requested a computer for her child to do class work and homework, but the IEP team does not agree. Kara complains to you. You should:**
    (Easy) (Skill 1.6)

    A. Tell her you agree with her.
    B. Recommend an outside source that may provide a free laptop computer.
    C. Tell Kara's mother she can still fight the team's decision by requesting a due process hearing.
    D. Tell the parent to call a lawyer.

Answer: C. Tell Kara's mother she can still fight the team's decision by requesting a due process hearing.

It is your legal obligation to let Kara's mother know that she does not have to accept the team decision if she does not like it, and that she can request a due process hearing.

60. **Shyquan is in your inclusive class, and she exhibits a slower comprehension of assigned tasks and concepts. Her first two grades were Bs, but she is now receiving failing marks. She has seen the resource teacher. You should:**
    (Rigorous) (Skill 1.7)

    A. Ask for a review of current placement.
    B. Tell Shyquan to seek extra help.
    C. Ask Shyquan if she is frustrated.
    D. Ask the regular education teacher to slow instruction.

Answer: A. Ask for a review of current placement

All of the responses listed above can be deemed correct, but you are responsible for reviewing her ability to function in the inclusive environment. Shyquan may or may not know she is not grasping the work, and she has sought out extra help with the resource teacher. Also, if the regular education class students are successful, the class should not be slowed to adjust to Shyquan's learning rate. It is more likely that she may require a more modified curriculum to stay on task and to succeed academically. This might require a more restrictive environment.

61. In exceptional student education, assessment is used to make decisions about all of the following except:
 (Average Rigor) (Skill 2.1)

   A. Screening and initial identification of children who may need services
   B. Selection and evaluation of teaching strategies and programs
   C. Determining the desired attendance rate of a student
   D. Development of goals, objectives, and evaluation for the IEP

Answer: C. Determining the desired attendance rate of a student

School attendance is required, and assessment is not necessary to measure a child's attendance rate.

62. The extent to which a test measures what it claims to measure is called: *(Easy) (Skill 2.3)*

   A. Reliability
   B. Validity
   C. Factor analysis
   D. Chi square

Answer: B. Validity

Validity is the degree to which a test measures what it claims to measure.

63. The purpose of error analysis of a test is to:
 (Easy) (Skill 2.3)

   A. Determine what events were labeled in error.
   B. Determine if the test length was the cause of error.
   C. Evaluate the types of errors made by categorizing incorrect answers.
   D. Establish a baseline.

Answer: C. Evaluate the types of errors made by categorizing incorrect answers.

Error analysis examines how and why a person makes a mistake. In an Informal Reading Inventory, such as those described by Burns and Roe (2002), questions are given to specifically address possible errors. Other tests that utilize error analysis provide specific possible answers to denote which error was made. The purpose of both is to see where problems lie and to provide clues to assist the learning process.

64. Which would NOT be an advantage of using a criterion-referenced test?
    (Easy) (Skill 2.3)

    A. You can use the results to evaluate the effectiveness of your teaching methods..
    B. It can pinpoint exact areas of weaknesses and strengths.
    C. You can design them yourself.
    D. You can compare your students to the national norm.

Answer: D. You can compare your students to the national norm.

Criterion-referenced tests measure mastery of content rather than performance compared to others. Test items are usually prepared from specific educational objectives and may be teacher made or commercially prepared. Scores are measured by the percentage of correct items for a skill (e.g., adding and subtracting fractions with like denominators). Such test can be used to evaluate teaching methods, as well as student mastery of objectives and individual student weaknesses and strengths, but they cannot be used to compare students to a norm. To do that you would need to use a norm referenced test.

65. Which is NOT an example of a standard score?
    (Average Rigor) (Skill 2.4)

    A. T score
    B. Z score
    C. Standard deviation
    D. Stanine

Answer: C. Standard deviation

A, B, and D are all standardized scores. Stanines are whole number scores from 1 to 9, each representing a wide range of raw scores. Standard deviation is not a score. It measures how widely scores vary from the mean.

TEACHER CERTIFICATION STUDY GUIDE

66. The most direct method of obtaining assessment data, and perhaps the most objective, is:
(Rigorous) (Skill 2.5)

   A. Testing
   B. Self-recording
   C. Observation
   D. Experimenting

Answer: C. Observation

Observation is often better than testing, due to language, culture, or other factors. It is also the most direct. All the others involve some intermediate step between observation and data.

67. The National Reading Panel Report (2000) reviewed research showing that direct instruction in vocabulary is essential, and that:
(Average Rigor) (Skill 5.15)

   A. Learning vocabulary in the specific context in which it is to be used is the most effective technique.
   B. Use of word maps is the most effective strategy for teaching vocabulary mastery.
   C. Using a variety of methods and approaches is far more effective than dependence upon a single approach to instruction.
   D. Noncontextual vocabulary strategies are the most effective methods for long term retention of vocabulary content.

Answer: C. Using a variety of methods and approaches is far more effective than dependence upon a single approach to instruction

Research shows not only that a variety of methods can be effective, but also that it is important to vary the methods used, both to keep student interest engaged, and also to suit the method to the specific type of vocabulary being learned. Methods shown to be effective include repetition and multiple exposures to vocabulary items; study of vocabulary that will be likely to appear in many contexts, learning vocabulary in context; ensuring that students are actively engaged in learning tasks; use of computer technology and educational software; repetition and drills with concrete, pictorial clues; an emphasis on multimedia aspects of vocabulary learning; applying vocabulary skills to writing as part of the lesson; and simply ensuring that students and teachers *talk about* words, their features, and how they are related.

68. **Alternative assessments include all of the following EXCEPT:**
    (Average Rigor) (Skill 2.5)

    A. Portfolios
    B. Interviews
    C. Standardized tests
    D. Performance Based Tests

Answer: C. Standardized tests

Standardized tests are formal, objective tests predominated by questions with one correct answer provided in only one way. Alternative assessments are flexible and allow students to respond in ways that maximize their learning and response style. As such, they cannot be standardized.

69. **Which of the following is NOT one of the three aspects of the issue of fair assessment for individuals from minority groups that Slavia and Ysseldyke, 1995, point out as particularly relevant to the assessment of students?**
    (Rigorous) (Skill 2.6)

    A. Representation
    B. Diversity
    C. Acculturation
    D. Language

Answer: B. Diversity

The issue of fair assessment for individuals from minority groups has a long history in the law, philosophy, and education. Individuals from diverse backgrounds need to be represented in assessment materials. It is also important that individuals from different backgrounds receive opportunities to acquire the tested skills, information, and values. The language and concepts that comprise test items should be unbiased, and students should be familiar with terminology and references to which the language is being made when they are administered tests, especially when the results of the tests are going to be used for decision-making purposes.

70. **The Premack Principle of increasing the performance of a less-preferred activity by immediately following it with a highly-preferred activity is the basis of:**
    (Rigorous) (Skill 3.2)

    A. Response cost
    B. Token systems
    C. Contingency contracting
    D. Self-recording management

Answer: C. Contingency contracting

In an unwritten contract, the student eagerly completes the less desirable activity to obtain the reward of the more desirable activity.

71. **A suggested amount of time for a large-group instruction lesson for a sixth- or seventh-grade group would be:**
    (Rigorous) (Skill 3.2)

    A. 5 to 40 minutes
    B. 5 to 50 minutes
    C. 5 to 30 minutes
    D. 5 to 15 minutes

Answer: C. 5 to 30 minutes

The recommended time for large group instruction is 5 - 15 minutes for grades 1-5, 5-30 for grades 6-7, and 5 – 40 minutes for grades 8-12.

72. **In a positive classroom environment, errors are viewed as:**
    (Easy) (Skill 3.2)

    A. Symptoms of deficiencies
    B. Lack of attention or ability
    C. A natural part of the learning process
    D. The result of going too fast

Answer: C. A natural part of the learning process

We often learn a great deal from our mistakes and shortcomings. It is normal. Where it is not normal, fear develops. This fear of failure inhibits children from taking risks to learn and achieve, and from working and achieving. Copying and other types of cheating result from this fear of failure.

TEACHER CERTIFICATION STUDY GUIDE

73. Which of the following should be considered when planning the spatial arrangement of your classroom?
    (Average Rigor) (Skill 3.2)

    A. Adequate physical space
    B. Lighting characteristics
    C. Window location
    D. All of the above

Answer: D. All of the above

All of these factors help determine whether the room is "invitational." . A classroom must have adequate physical space so students can conduct themselves comfortably. Some students are distracted by windows, doors, pencil sharpeners, etc. The space must be organized in a manner that makes it easier for students to carry out their daily tasks.

Adequate lighting is also important. Flickering lights can produce headaches in children with latent epilepsy, and some students are very sensitive to the glare from florescent lights and will need shades or desk lamps to compensate.

Ventilation and climate control are particularly relevant for students with Autism spectrum disorders, who may be extremely sensitive to odors, or students with asthma who react badly to dusty or stuffy rooms.

Warmer subdued colors contribute to students' concentration on task items. Neutral hues for coloration of walls, ceiling, and carpet or tile are generally used in classrooms so distraction because of classroom coloration may be minimized.

74. Cooperative learning does NOT utilize?
    (Average Rigor) (Skill 3.2)

    A. Shared ideas
    B. Small groups
    C. Independent practice
    D. Student expertise

Answer: C. Independent practice

Cooperative learning focuses on group cooperation, allowing for sharing of student expertise, and provides some flexibility for creative presentations of the students as they share with others.

TEACHER CERTIFICATION STUDY GUIDE

75. **Which type of grouping arrangement would be MOST effective for teaching basic academic skills such as math facts or reading?**
    (Rigorous) (Skill 3.2)

    A. Large group with teacher
    B. Peer tutoring
    C. Small group instruction
    D. Cooperative learning

Answer: C. Small group instruction

Small group instruction usually includes 5 to 7 students and is recommended for teaching basic academic skills such as math facts or reading. This model is especially effective for students with learning problems. Large-group instruction is time efficient and prepares students for higher levels of secondary and post-secondary education settings. However, with large groups, instruction cannot be as easily tailored to high or low levels of students. In an effective peer tutoring arrangement, the teacher trains the peer tutors and matches them with students who need extra practice and assistance. Cooperative learning differs from peer tutoring in that students are grouped in teams or small groups, and the methods are based on teamwork, individual accountability, and team reward.

76. **If the arrangement in a fixed-ratio schedule of reinforcement is 3, when will the student receive the reinforcer?**
    (Rigorous) (Skill 3.3)

    A. After every third correct response
    B. After every third correct response in a row
    C. After the third correct response in the time interval of the behavior sample
    D. After the third correct response even if the undesired behavior occurs in between correct responses

Answer: B. After every third correct response in a row

A fixed ratio schedule of reinforcement provides reinforcement after every third correct response in a row. It produces a steady, efficient production of responses with only a slight pause after reinforcement.

77. **Laura is beginning to raise her hand first instead of talking out. An effective schedule of reinforcement should be:**
    (Rigorous) (Skill 3.3)

    A. Continuous
    B. Variable
    C. Intermittent
    D. Fixed

Answer: A. Continuous

The pattern of reinforcement should not be variable, intermittent, or fixed. It should be continuous. Continuous reinforcement forms a strong relationship between the behavior and the reinforcement. It is best for establishing a new habit.

78. **As Laura continues to raise her hand to speak, the teacher would want to change to this schedule of reinforcement in order to wean her from the reinforcement:**
    (Rigorous) (Skill 3.3)

    A. Continuous
    B. Variable
    C. Intermittent
    D. Fixed

Answer: D. Fixed

The pattern should be in a fixed ratio. This schedule of reinforcement produces a high, steady rate of responding to solidify new habits and resist extinction.

TEACHER CERTIFICATION STUDY GUIDE

79. **Laura has demonstrated that she has mastered the goal of raising her hand to speak; reinforcement during the maintenance phase should be:**
    (Rigorous) (Skill 3.3)

    A. Continuous
    B. Variable
    C. Intermittent
    D. Fixed

Answer: C. Intermittent

Reinforcement should be intermittent, as the behavior is now established and needs only minimum reward periodically for maintenance.

80. **A student may have great difficulty in meeting a target goal if the teacher has not first considered:**
    (Rigorous) (Skill 3.3)

    A. If the student has external or internal locus of control
    B. If the student is motivated to attain the goal
    C. If the student has the essential prerequisite skills to perform the goal
    D. If the student has had previous success or failure meeting the goal in other classes

Answer: C. If the student has the essential prerequisite skills to perform the goal

Prerequisite skills are essential in both setting goals and attaining goals.

81. **Justin, a second grader, is reinforced if he is on task at the end of each 10-minute block of time that the teacher observes him. This is an example of what type of schedule?**
    (Average Rigor) (Skill 3.3)

    A. Continuous
    B. Fixed interval
    C. Fixed-rat
    D. Variable ratio

Answer: B. Fixed interval

10 minutes is a fixed interval of time.

82. At the beginning of the school year, Annette had a problem with being late for class. Her teacher reinforced her each time she was in her seat when the bell rang. In October, her teacher decided to reward her every other day when she was not tardy to class. This reinforcement schedule would be:
   (Rigorous) (Skill 3.3)

   A. Continuous
   B. Fixed interval
   C. Variable ratio
   D. Fixed ratio

Answer: B. Fixed interval

Every other day is a fixed interval of time and is appropriate for making the transition to maintenance.

83. By November, Annette's teacher is satisfied with her record of being on time and decides to change the schedule of reinforcement. The best type of reinforcement schedule for maintenance of behavior is:
   (Average Rigor) (Skill 3.3)

   A. Continuous
   B. Fixed interval
   C. Variable ratio
   D. Fixed ratio

Answer: C. Variable ratio

Variable produce behavior more resistant to extinction than continuous schedules, and ratio schedules are more resistant than intervals, so a variable ratio will help reduce the chances of extinction and maintain the behavior.

84. **Transfer of learning occurs when?**
    (Rigorous) (Skill 3.3)

    A. Experience with one task influences performance on another task.
    B. Content can be explained orally.
    C. Student experiences the "I got it!" syndrome.
    D. Curricular objective is exceeded.

Answer: A. Experience with one task influences performance on another task.

Transfer of learning occurs when experience with one task influences performance on another task. Positive transfer occurs when the required responses are about the same and the stimuli are similar, such as moving from baseball to handball to racquetball or from field hockey to soccer. Negative transfer occurs when the stimuli remain similar, but the required responses change, such as shifting from soccer to football, tennis to racquetball, and boxing to sports karate.

85. **To facilitate learning instructional objectives:**
    (Average Rigor) (Skill 3.3)

    A. should be taken from a grade-level spelling list.
    B. should be written and shared.
    C. should be arranged in order of similarity.
    D. should be taken from a scope and sequence.

Answer: C. They should be arranged in order of similarity.

To facilitate learning, instructional objectives should be arranged in order according to their patterns of similarity. Objectives involving similar responses should be closely sequenced; thus, the possibility for positive transfer is stressed. Likewise, learning objectives that involve different responses should be programmed within instructional procedures in the most appropriate way possible. In all cases, objectives that are prerequisites for success in *other* objectives must be taught first.

86. Marisol has been mainstreamed into a ninth grade language arts class. Although her behavior is satisfactory, and she likes the class, Marisol's reading level is about two years below grade level. The class has been assigned to read *Great Expectations* and to write a report. What intervention would be LEAST successful in helping Marisol complete this assignment?
(Average Rigor) (Skill 3.5)

   A. Having Marisol listen to a taped recording while following the story in the regular text
   B. Giving her a modified version of the story
   C. Telling her to choose a different book that she can read
   D. Showing a film to the entire class and comparing and contrasting it with the book

Answer: C. Telling her to choose a different book that she can read

A, B, and D are positive interventions. C is not a productive intervention. In addition, it effectively *removes her from the rest of the class,* and **denies** her **access** to the same curriculum the other students have. The other interventions constitute valid accommodations that allow her to access the same curriculum the students without disabilities have.

87. Teacher modeling, student-teacher dialogues, and peer interactions are part of which teaching technique designed to provide support during the initial stages of instruction?
(Rigorous) (Skill 3.5)

   A. Reciprocal teaching
   B. Scaffolding
   C. Peer tutoring
   D. Cooperative learning

Answer: B. Scaffolding

Scaffolding, as the name implies, provides support to assist in the early stages of new learning.

TEACHER CERTIFICATION STUDY GUIDE

88. **Grading should be based on all of the following EXCEPT:**
    (Average Rigor) (Skill 3.5)

    A. Clearly-defined mastery of course objectives
    B. A variety of evaluation methods
    C. Performance of the student in relation to other students
    D. Assigning points for activities and basing grades on a point total

Answer: C. Performance of the student in relation to other students

Grading should never be based on the comparisons with the performance of other students. It should always be based on the student's mastery of course objectives, the methods of evaluation, and the grading rubric (how points are assigned).

89. **Which of the following sentences will NOT test recall?**
    (Average Rigor) (Skill 3.5)

    A. What words in the story describe Goldilocks?
    B. Why did Goldilocks go into the three bears' house?
    C. Name in order the things that belonged to the three bears that Goldilocks tried.
    D. What did the three bears learn about leaving their house unlocked?

Answer: D. What did the three bears learn about leaving their house unlocked?

Recall requires the student to produce from memory ideas and information explicitly stated in the story. Answer D. requires an inference.

90. **Which is not a goal of collaborative consultation?**
    (Average Rigor) (Skill 3.6)

    A. Prevent learning and behavior problems with mainstreamed students
    B. Coordinate the instructional programs between mainstream and Exceptional Student Education (ESE) classes
    C. Facilitate solutions to learning and behavior problems
    D. Function as an ESE service model

Answer: D. Function as an ESE service model

A, B, and C are goals. Functioning as an exceptional student education model is not a goal. Collaborative consultation is necessary for the classification of students with disabilities and provision of services to satisfy their needs.

TEACHER CERTIFICATION STUDY GUIDE

91. An important goal of collaborative consultation is:
    (Easy) (Skill 3.6)

    A. Mainstream as many ESE students as possible
    B. Guidance on how to handle ESE students from the ESE teacher
    C. Mutual empowerment of both the mainstream and the ESE teacher
    D. Document progress of mainstreamed students

Answer: C. Mutual empowerment of both the mainstream and the ESE teacher

Empowerment of these service providers is extremely important.

92. Knowledge of evaluation strategies, program interventions, and types of data are examples of which variable for a successful consultation program?
    (Average Rigor) (Skill 3.6)

    A. People
    B. Process
    C. Procedural implementation
    D. Academic preparation

Answer: B. Process

Consultation programs cannot be successful without knowledge of the process.

93. Skills as an administrator and background in client, consulter, and consultation skills are examples of which variable in a successful consultation program?
    (Average Rigor) (Skill 3.6)

    A. People
    B. Process
    C. Procedural implementation
    D. Academic preparation

Answer: A. People

Consultation programs cannot be successful without people skills.

94. The ability to identify problems, generate solutions, and knowledge of theoretical perspectives of consultation are examples of which variable in a successful consultation program?
    (Average Rigor) (Skill 3.6)

    A. People
    B. Process
    C. Procedural implementation
    D. Academic preparation

Answer: C. Procedural implementation

Consultation programs cannot be successful without implementation skills.

95. A serious hindrance to successful mainstreaming is:
    (Average Rigor) (Skill 3.6)

    A. Lack of adapted materials
    B. Lack of funding
    C. Lack of communication among teachers
    D. Lack of support from administration

Answer: C. Lack of communication among teachers

All 4 choices are hindrances, but lack of communication and consultation between the service providers is serious.

96. Mrs. Taylor takes her students to a special gymnastics presentation that the P.E. coach has arranged in the gym. She has a rule against talk-outs and reminds the students that they will lose 5 points on their daily point sheet for talking out. The students get a chance to perform some of the simple stunts. They all easily go through the movements except for Sam, who is known as the class klutz. Sam does not give up and finally completes the stunts. His classmates cheer him on with comments like, "Way to go!" Their teacher, however, reminds them that they broke the no talking rule and will lose the points. What mistake was made here?
(Average Rigor) (Skill 3.6)

   A. The students forgot the no talking rule.
   B. The teacher considered talk-outs to be maladaptive in all school settings.
   C. The other students could have distracted Sam with talk-outs and caused him to get hurt.
   D. The teacher should have let the P.E. coach handle the discipline in the gym.

Answer: D. The teacher should have let the P.E. coach handle the discipline in the gym.

The gym environment is different from a classroom environment. The class encouragement was, in fact, a positive example of cooperative learning and support. The teacher let the "letter of the law" take precedence over more important educational and behavioral goals. The gym teacher's rules would have been designed to keep the environment safe. It was counter productive and inappropriate to use a rule designed for the classroom in this setting.

97. A student on medication may have his/her dosage adjusted as his/her body grows. Parents may call and ask questions about their child's adjustment to the medication during the school day. During this time you should:
    (Average Rigor) (Skill 3.6)

    A. Observe the student for changes in behavior.
    B. Watch for a progression of changed behavior.
    C. Communicate with the parent concerns about sleepiness.
    D. All of the above

Answer: D. All of the above

If you have students on medication, it is important to communicate with the parents about any changes in behavior, because their bodies are constantly growing. Being informed about the medication(s) your students are on allows you to assist the students and the parents as an objective observer.

98. You are having continual difficulty with your classroom assistant. A good strategy to address this problem would be:
    (Rigorous) (Skill 3.6)

    A. To address the issue immediately
    B. To take away responsibilities
    C. To write a clearly-established role plan to discuss
    D. To speak to your supervisor

Answer: C. To write a clearly-established role plan to discuss

If you are having difficulty with your classroom assistant, it is most likely over an issue or issues that have happened repeatedly, and you have attempted to address them. Establishing clear roles between the two of you will provide a good step in the right direction. It may also provide you with the ability to state that you have made an attempt to address the issue/issues to an administrator should the need arise.

99. **A consultant teacher should be meeting the needs of his/her students by:**
    (Easy) (Skill 3.6)

    A. Pushing in to do small-group instruction with regular education students
    B. Asking the student to show his/her reasoning for failing
    C. Meeting with the teacher before class to discuss adaptations and expectations
    D. Accompanying the student to class

Answer: A. Pushing in to do small-group instruction with regular education students

Students that receive consult services are receiving minimum instructional services. They require little modification to their educational program, and these modifications should take place in the general education classroom.

100. **Parent contact should first begin when:**
     (Average Rigor) (Skill 3.6)

     A. You are informed the child will be your student.
     B. The student fails a test.
     C. The student exceeds others on a task.
     D. A CSE is coming, and you have had no previous replies to letters.

Answer: A. You are informed the child will be your student.

Student contact should begin as a getting to know you piece, which allows you to begin on a non-judgmental platform. It also allows the parent to receive a view that you are a professional who is willing to work with them.

101. Parents of children with disabilities may seek your advice on several aspects regarding their child. A mother calls you and complains she can't keep her son on task so much that she has to keep sending her son back to the bathroom until he finishes getting prepared for the day. What advice should you give her?
(Average Rigor) (Skill 3.6)

   A. Request an educational evaluation.
   B. Recommend close supervision until he does all tasks together consistently.
   C. Create a list of tasks to be completed in the bathroom.
   D. Ask for outside coordination of services advocacy that can assist with this type of issue.

Answer: C. Create a list of tasks to be completed in the bathroom.

The child is independent on each task. Calling outside resources is a good idea, but it does not address the issue. The student may simply have a short-term memory loss and may need a reminder to keep on task.

102. Which of the following is NOT an appropriate assessment modification or accommodation for a student with a learning disability?
(Average Rigor) (Skill 3.7)

   A. Having the test read orally to the student
   B. Writing down the student's dictated answers
   C. Allowing the student to take the assessment home to complete
   D. Extending the time for the student to take the assessment

Answer: C. Allowing the student to take the assessment home to complete

Unless a student is homebound, the student should take assessments in class or in another classroom setting. All the other items listed are appropriate accommodations.

TEACHER CERTIFICATION STUDY GUIDE

103. **Which of the following is NOT one of the four interrelated components of positive behavioral interventions and supports (PBS)?**
     (Rigorous) (Skill 4.1)

    A. Systems change activities
    B. Environmental alterations activities
    C. Behavioral consequences activities
    D. Support provision activities

Answer: D. Support provision activities

Positive behavioral interventions and supports (PBS) is IDEA's preferred strategy for handling challenging behaviors of students with disabilities. IDEA requires PBS to be considered in all cases of students whose behavior impedes their learning or the learning of others. PBS involves the use of positive behavioral interventions and systems to attain socially significant behavior change. PBS has four interrelated components. The components are as follows: systems change activities, environmental alterations activities, skill instruction activities, and behavioral consequence activities.

104. **Examples of behaviors that are appropriate to be monitored by measuring duration include all EXCEPT:**
     (Average Rigor) (Skill 4.2)

    A. Thumb sucking
    B. Hitting
    C. Temper tantrums
    D. Maintaining eye contact

Answer: B. Hitting

Hitting takes place in an instant. This should be measured by frequency.

105. **Examples of behaviors that are appropriate to be monitored by measuring frequency include all EXCEPT:**
    (Average Rigor) (Skill 4.2)

    A. Teasing
    B. Talking out
    C. Being on time for class
    D. Off task behavior

Answer: D. Off task behavior

Off task behavior is relevant to learning because it reduces time on task or engaged time, therefore, it should be measured by duration. It is the duration of the behavior that is most important.

106. **Criteria for choosing behaviors to measure by frequency include all but those that:**
    (Easy) (Skill 4.2)

    A. Have an observable beginning
    B. Last a long time
    C. Last a short time
    D. Occur often

Answer: B. Last a long time

We use frequency to measure behaviors that do not last a long time, but do have observable beginnings and ends.

107. **Criteria for choosing behaviors to measure by duration include all but those that:**
    (Easy) (Skill 4.2)

    A. Last a short time
    B. Last a long time
    C. Have no readily observable beginning or end
    D. Don't happen often

Answer: A. Last a short time

We use duration to measure behaviors that tend to last a longer time or for which duration is the key dimension (see #105).

TEACHER CERTIFICATION STUDY GUIDE

108. Data on quiet behaviors, e.g., nail biting or daydreaming, are best measured using a/an:
     (Rigorous) (Skill 4.2)

     A. Interval or time sample
     B. Continuous sample
     C. Variable sample
     D. Fixed-ratio sample

Answer: A. Interval or time sample

An interval or time sample is best to measure the duration of these behaviors because they are not easily noticed and it may be difficult to find beginning and ending times.

109. Mr. Jones wants to design an intervention for reducing Jason's sarcastic remarks. He wants to find out who or what is reinforcing Jason's remarks, so he records data on Jason's behavior, as well as the attending behavior of his peers. This is an example of collecting data on:
     (Rigorous) (Skill 4.2)

     A. Reciprocal behaviors
     B. Multiple behaviors for single subjects
     C. Single behaviors for multiple subjects
     D. Qualitative data on Jason

Answer: A. Reciprocal behaviors

Jason's peers' behaviors are in response to Jason's disruptive behaviors. His behavior is related to theirs and theirs to his—a reciprocal relationship.

110. **Ms. Beekman has a class of students who frequently talk out. She wishes to begin interventions with the students who are talking out the most. She monitors the talking behavior of the entire class for 1-minute samples every half-hour. This is an example of collecting data on:**
(Rigorous) (Skill 4.2)

   A. Multiple behaviors for single subjects
   B. Reciprocal behaviors
   C. Single behaviors for multiple subjects
   D. Continuous behaviors for fixed intervals

Answer: C. Single behaviors for multiple subjects

Talking out is the only behavior being observed, but she is recording it for multiple subjects.

111. **Statements like, "Darren is lazy," are not helpful in describing his behavior for all but which of these reasons?**
(Rigorous) (Skill 4.2)

   A. There is no way to determine if any change occurs from the information given.
   B. The student and not the behavior is being labeled.
   C. Darren's behavior will manifest itself clearly enough without any written description.
   D. Constructs are open to various interpretations among the people who are asked to define them.

Answer: C. Darren's behavior will manifest itself clearly enough without any written description.

'Darren is lazy' is a label of the child, not the behavior. Even were the label more appropriately applied to the behavior, it can be interpreted in a variety of ways, and there is no way to measure this description for change. A description should be measurable.

112. Marcie often is not in her seat when the bell rings. She may be found at the pencil sharpener, throwing paper away, or fumbling through her notebook. Which of these descriptions of her behavior can be described as a pinpoint?
    (Average Rigor) (Skill 4.2)

    A. Is tardy a lot
    B. Is out of seat
    C. Is not in seat when the late bell rings
    D. Is disorganized

Answer: C. Is not in seat when late bell rings

Even though A, B, and D describe the behavior, C is most precise.

113. Which of the following should be avoided when writing objectives for social behavior?
    (Easy) (Skill 4.2)

    A. Non-specific adverbs
    B. Behaviors stated as verbs
    C. Criteria for acceptable performance
    D. Conditions where the behavior is expected to be performed

Answer: A. Non-specific adverbs

Behaviors should be specific. The more clearly the behavior is described, the less the chance for error.

TEACHER CERTIFICATION STUDY GUIDE

114. Criteria for choosing behaviors that are in the most need of change involve all but the following:
     (Average Rigor) (Skill 4.2)

    A. Observations across settings to rule out certain interventions
    B. Pinpointing the behavior that is the poorest fit in the child's environment
    C. The teacher's concern about what is the most important behavior to target
    D. Analysis of the environmental reinforcers

Answer: C. The teacher's concern about what is the most important behavior to target

A, B, and D are more objective measures of the behavior and its effects. As such, it is these that should be the focus of the teacher's efforts, rather than the teacher's personal concerns or interpretations.

115. Anecdotal records should:
     (Average Rigor) (Skill 4.2)

    A. Record observable behavior
    B. End with conjecture
    C. Record motivational factors
    D. Note previously-stated interests

Answer: A. Record observable behavior

Anecdotal records should only record observable behavior, describing the actions, and not possible interest or motivational factors that may lead to possible prejudicial reviews.

116. Mr. Brown finds that his chosen consequence does not seem to be having the desired effect of reducing the target misbehavior. Which of these would LEAST LIKELY account for Mr. Brown's lack of success with the consequence?
(Average Rigor) (Skill 4.3)

   A. The consequence was aversive in Mr. Brown's opinion but not the students'.
   B. The students were not developmentally ready to understand the connection.
   C. Mr. Brown was inconsistent in applying the consequence.
   D. The intervention had not previously been shown to be effective in studies.

Answer: D. The intervention had not previously been shown to be effective in studies.

A, B, and C might work if applied in the classroom, but research is the least of Mr. Brown's options.

117. Which of the following is NOT a feature of effective classroom rules?
(Easy) (Skill 4.3)

   A. They are about 4 to 6 in number.
   B. They are negatively stated.
   C. Consequences are consistent and immediate.
   D. They can be tailored to individual teaching goals and teaching styles.

Answer: B. They are negatively stated.

Rules should be positively stated, and they should follow the other three features listed.

118. **Ms. Wright is planning an analysis of Audrey's out-of-seat behavior. Her initial data would be called:**
    (Rigorous) (Skill 4.3)

    A. Pre-referral phase
    B. Intervention phase
    C. Baseline phase
    D. Observation phase

Answer: C. Baseline phase

Ms Wright is a teacher. She should begin at the baseline phase, describing the behavior before any interventions are applied. Without a baseline, it is impossible to quantify and changes in behavior or to evaluate the interventions.

119. **To reinforce Audrey each time she is on task and in her seat, Ms. Wright delivers specific praise and stickers, which Audrey may collect and redeem for a reward. The data collected during the time Ms. Wright is using this intervention is called:**
    (Easy) (Skill 4.3)

    A. Referral phase
    B. Intervention phase
    C. Baseline phase
    D. Observation phase

Answer: B. Intervention phase

Ms Wright is involved in behavior modification. This is the intervention phase; she has applied an intervention (reinforcement).

120. **Crisis intervention methods are concerned above all with:**
    (Easy) (Skill 4.4)

    A. Safety and well being of the staff and students
    B. Stopping the inappropriate behavior
    C. Preventing the behavior from occurring again
    D. The student learning that outbursts are inappropriate

Answer: A. Safety and well being of the staff and students

It encompasses B, C, and D.

TEACHER CERTIFICATION STUDY GUIDE

121. Ricky, a third-grade student, runs out of the classroom and onto the roof of the school. He paces around the roof, looks around to see who is watching, and laughs at the people on the ground. He appears to be in control of his behavior. What should the teacher do?
(Average Rigor) (Skill 4.4)

   A. Go back inside and leave him up there until he decides he is ready to come down.
   B. Climb up to get Ricky so he does not fall off and get hurt.
   C. Notify the crisis teacher and arrange to have someone monitor Ricky.
   D. Call the police.

Answer: C. Notify the crisis teacher and arrange to have someone monitor Ricky.

The teacher cannot be responsible for both Ricky and his or her class. He must pass the responsibility to the appropriate person.

122. Mr. Smith is on a field trip with a group of high school EH students. On the way, they stop at a fast-food restaurant for lunch, and Warren and Raul get into a disagreement. After some heated words, Warren stalks out of the restaurant and refuses to return to the group. He leaves the parking lot, continues walking away from the group, and ignores Mr. Smith's directions to come back. What would be the best course of action for Mr. Smith?
(Average Rigor) (Skill 4.4)

   A. Leave the group with the class aide and follow Warren to try to talk him into coming back.
   B. Wait a little while and see if Warren cools off and returns.
   C. Telephone the school and let the crisis teacher notify the police in accordance with school policy.
   D. Call the police himself.

Answer: C. Telephone the school and let the crisis teacher notify the police in accordance with school policy.

Mr. Smith is still responsible for his class. This is his only option.

123. **An effective classroom behavior management plan includes all EXCEPT which of the following?**
    (Easy) (Skill 4.4)

    A. Transition procedures for changing activities
    B. Clear consequences for rule infractions
    C. Concise teacher expectations for student behavior
    D. Copies of lesson plans

Answer: D. Copies of lesson plans

D is not a part of any behavior management plan. A, B, and C are.

124. **Which of these would be the LEAST effective measure of behavioral disorders?**
    (Easy) (Skill 4.4)

    A. Projective test
    B. Ecological assessment
    C. Achievement test
    D. Psychodynamic analysis

Answer: C. Achievement test

Achievement tests measure mastery of specific skills, not behavioral variables or disorders..

125. **When a teacher is choosing behaviors to modify, two issues must be considered. What are they?**
    (Average Rigor) (Skill 4.4)

    A. The need for the behavior to be performed in public and the culture of acceptance
    B. The culture of the child and society standards regarding the behavior
    C. Evidence that the behavior can be changed and society norms
    D. Standards of the student's community and school rules

Answer: B. The culture of the child and society standards regarding the behavior

American society standards may/may not be the same as standards of other cultures. It may be important to check the standards of the specific behavior in the student's cultural background before attempting to modify it.

TEACHER CERTIFICATION STUDY GUIDE

126. **According to IDEA 2004, a FBA must be:**
     (Average Rigor) (Skill 4.4)

    A. Written by the special education administrator
    B. Written by the teacher who has the issue with the student
    C. Written by the primary teacher
    D. Written by a team

Answer: D. Written by a team

FBAs (Functional Behavioral Assessments) should be written and reviewed as a team. This approach is the most effective for improving student behavior.

127. **Which is the LEAST effective of reinforcers in programs for mildly to moderately handicapped learners?**
     (Average Rigor) (Skill 4.5)

    A. Tokens
    B. Social
    C. Food
    D. Activity

Answer: C. Food

Food is the least effective reinforcer for most handicapped children. Tokens, social interaction, or activity are more desirable. Food may have reached satiation.

128. **Teacher feedback, task completion, and a sense of pride over mastery or accomplishment of a skill are examples of:**
     (Average Rigor) (Skill 4.5)

    A. Extrinsic reinforcers
    B. Behavior modifiers
    C. Intrinsic reinforcers
    D. Positive feedback

Answer: C. Intrinsic reinforcers

Motivation may be achieved through intrinsic reinforcers or extrinsic reinforcers. Intrinsic reinforcers are usually intangible, and extrinsic reinforcers are usually tangible rewards and from an external source. These are intangibles.

129. Social approval, token reinforcers, and rewards, such as pencils or stickers, are examples of:
   (Average Rigor) (Skill 4.5)

   A. Extrinsic reinforcers
   B. Behavior modifiers
   C. Intrinsic reinforcers
   D. Positive feedback reinforcers

Answer: A. Extrinsic reinforcers

These are rewards from external sources.

130. Token systems are popular for all of these advantages EXCEPT:
   (Average Rigor) (Skill 4.5)

   A. The number needed for rewards may be adjusted as needed.
   B. Rewards are easy to maintain.
   C. They are effective for students who generally do not respond to social reinforcers.
   D. Tokens reinforce the relationship between desirable behavior and reinforcement.

Answer: B. Rewards are easy to maintain.

The ease of maintenance is not a valid reason for developing a token system.

131. Skilled readers use all EXCEPT which one of these knowledge sources to construct meanings beyond the literal text:
   (Rigorous) (Skill 5.1)

   A. Text knowledge
   B. Syntactic knowledge
   C. Morphological knowledge
   D. Semantic knowledge

Answer: C. Morphological knowledge

The student is already skilled, so morphological knowledge is already in place.

132. Indirect requests and attempts to influence or control others through one's use of language is an example of:
    (Rigorous) (Skill 5.1)

    A. Morphology
    B. Syntax
    C. Pragmatics
    D. Semantics

Answer: C. Pragmatics

Pragmatics involves the way that language is used to communicate and interact with others. It is often used to control the actions and attitudes of people.

133. Kenny, a fourth grader, has trouble comprehending analogies, using comparative, spatial, and temporal words, and multiple meanings. Language interventions for Kenny would focus on:
    (Rigorous) (Skill 5.1)

    A. Morphology
    B. Syntax
    C. Pragmatics
    D. Semantics

Answer: D. Semantics

Semantics has to do with word and sentence meanings. Semantic tests measure receptive and expressive vocabulary skills.

134. Celia, who is in first grade, asked, "Where are my ball?" She also has trouble with passive sentences. Language interventions for Celia would target:
    (Rigorous) (Skill 5.1)

    A. Morphology
    B. Syntax
    C. Pragmatics
    D. Semantics

Answer: B. Syntax

Syntax refers to the rules for arranging words to make sentences.

140. When a student begins to use assistive technology, it is important for the teacher to have a clear outline as to when and how the equipment should be used. Why?
(Rigorous) (Skill 5.4)

   A. To establish a level of accountability with the student
   B. To establish that the teacher has responsibility of the equipment that is in use in his/her room
   C. To establish that the teacher is responsible for the usage of the assistive technology
   D. To establish a guideline for evaluation

Answer: A. To establish a level of accountability with the student

Clear parameters as to the usage of assistive technology in a classroom create a level of accountability in the student, as he/she now knows the teacher knows the intended purpose and appropriate manner of use of the device.

141. Sam is working to earn half an hour of basketball time with his favorite P.E. teacher. At the end of each half hour, Sam marks his point sheet with an X if he reached his goal of no call-outs. When he has received 25 marks, he will receive his basketball free time. This behavior management strategy is an example of:
(Average Rigor) (Skill 6.1)

   A. Self-recording
   B. Self-evaluation
   C. Self-reinforcement
   D. Self-regulation

Answer: A. Self-recording

Self-Management is an important part of social skills training, especially for older students preparing for employment. Components for self-management include: *self-monitoring:* choosing behaviors and alternatives and monitoring those actions; *self-evaluation:* deciding the effectiveness of the behavior in solving the problem; and *self-reinforcement:* telling oneself that one is capable of achieving success. Sam is recording his behavior.

142. Mark has been working on his target goal of completing his mathematics class work. Each day he records, on a scale of 0 to 3, how well he has done his work, and his teacher provides feedback. This self-management technique is an example of:
    (Average Rigor) (Skill 6.1)

    A. Self-recording
    B. Self-reinforcement
    C. Self-regulation
    D. Self-evaluation

Answer: D. Self-evaluation

Sam is evaluating his behavior, not merely recording it.

143. When Barbara reached her target goal, she chose her reinforcer and said softly to herself, "I worked hard, and I deserve this reward." This self-management technique is an example of:
    (Average Rigor) (Skill 6.1)

    A. Self-reinforcement
    B. Self-recording
    C. Self-regulation
    D. Self-evaluation

Answer: A. Self-reinforcement

Barbara is reinforcing her behavior.

144. Teaching children functional skills that will be useful in their home life and neighborhoods is the basis of:
    (Rigorous) (Skill 6.1)

    A. Curriculum-based instruction
    B. Community-based instruction
    C. Transition planning
    D. Functional curriculum

Answer: B. Community-based instruction

Teaching functional skills in the wider curriculum is considered community-based instruction.

145. **Measurement of adaptive behavior should include all EXCEPT:** *(Rigorous) (Skill 6.1)*

    A. Student's behavior in a variety of settings
    B. Student's skills displayed in a variety of settings
    C. Comparative analysis to other students in his/her class
    D. Analysis of student's social skills

Answer: C. Comparative analysis to other students in his/her class

Evaluating a student's adaptability requires analysis only of that person and does not allow for comparative analysis. Comparing oneself to others or comparing skill levels is not a good measure of adaptability. The target is the adaptive behavior, not how the student compares to others.

146. **Functional curriculum focuses on all of the following EXCEPT:** *(Rigorous) (Skill 6.1)*

    A. Skills needed for social living
    B. Occupational readiness
    C. Functioning in society
    D. Remedial academic skills

Answer: D. Remedial academic skills

Remedial academics may be applied but are not a focus. The primary goal is to achieve skills for functioning in society, if possible, on an independent basis.

TEACHER CERTIFICATION STUDY GUIDE

147. **In order to effectively differentiate instruction, the teacher must do all of the following EXCEPT:**
     (Average Rigor) (Skill 3.5)

    A. Assess where individual students are with reference to an objective
    B. Design some lesson material that addresses the objective at a cognitively less demanding level
    C. Assess all students uniformly, on the same set of standards
    D. Design some lesson material that addresses the objective on a more advanced level

    Answer: C. Assess all students uniformly on the same set of standards.

    In planning differentiated instruction, teachers must first determine where the students *are* with reference to an objective, *then* tailor specific lesson plans and learning activities to help each student learn as much as possible about that objective. The *content* of the lesson must be varied to include varying levels of cognitive demand depending upon student need. For some students a lower or entry level of the objective must be determined, for others, advanced applications and higher level thinking tasks must be developed. For most, the objective as stated in the standards can be taught for mastery. In addition, the *process* by which the objective is taught should be altered to meet different student need, and the method of assessment may need to be similarly modified.

148. **A student with a poor self-concept may manifest in all of the ways listed below EXCEPT:**
     (Average Rigor) (Skill 6.3)

    A. Withdrawn actions
    B. Aggression
    C. Consistently announcing his/her achievements
    D. Shyness.

    Answer: C. Consistently announcing his/her achievements

    A poor self-concept is not common in someone who boasts of his/her achievements.

149. Career exploration involves all of the following activities EXCEPT: (Rigorous) (Skill 7.1)

   A. Listening to guest speakers
   B. Contextual learning activities
   C. Simulated work experiences
   D. Job shadowing

Answer: A. Listening to guest speakers

Career exploration focuses on learning about careers through direct, hands-on activities. In-school activities include contextual learning activities, simulated work experiences, and career fairs. Work-based experiences range from non-paid to paid activities. These activities include job shadowing, mentors, company tours, internships, service learning, cooperative education, and independent study. Listening to guest speakers falls into the Career Awareness component of career education.

150. The transition activities that have to be addressed, unless the IEP team finds it uncalled for, include all of the following EXCEPT: (Rigorous) (Skill 7.2)

   A. Instruction
   B. Volunteer opportunities
   C. Community experiences
   D. Development of objectives related to employment and other post-school areas

Answer: B. Volunteer opportunities

Volunteer opportunities, although worthwhile, are not listed as one of the three transition activities that have to be addressed on a student's IEP.

More Study Tools to Help Pass Your Certification Exam

XAMonline.com

Pass your exam with our suite of superior study tools, including:

- Print books
- eBooks
- eFlashcards
- Web-based interactive study guides

Teaching in another state? XAMonline carries 500+ state-specific and PRAXIS study guides covering every test subject nationwide.

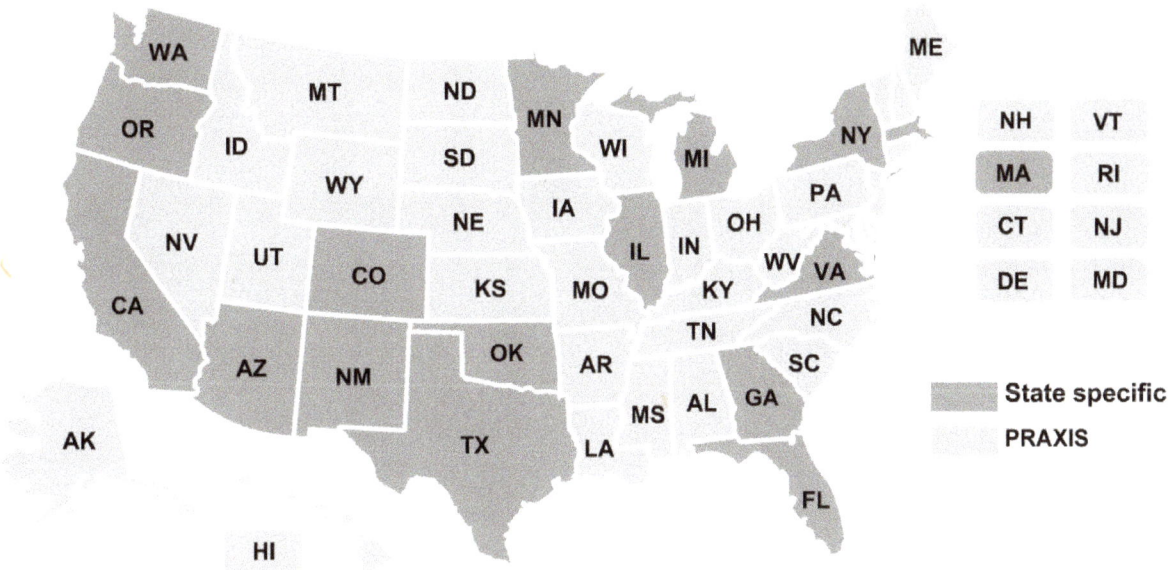

Call or visit us online!
800.301.4647 | www.XAMonline.com

www.ingramcontent.com/pod-product-compliance
Lightning Source LLC
Chambersburg PA
CBHW062129160426
43191CB00013B/2247